CONTENTS

There is no neutral personal pronoun in English, so to avoid the awkwardness of using 'he or she' when both sexes are intended, I have used the feminine form arbitrarily. I have no wish to suggest that men do not make as good storytellers as women, for the contrary is my experience! The advice I have given applies both to men and women.

STORYTELLING

EILEEN COLWELL

Storytelling

THE BODLEY HEAD
LONDON SYDNEY
TORONTO

In memory of U.C., who loved to
listen to my stories and whose
professional knowledge helped
me in the telling of them.

British Library Cataloguing
in Publication Data
Colwell, Eileen
Storytelling. 1. Story-telling
I. Title
808.5'43   LB1042
ISBN 0-370-30228-1

Printed in Great Britain for
The Bodley Head Ltd
9 Bow Street, London WC2E 7AL
by Redwood Burn Ltd,
Trowbridge & Esher
Phototypeset in V.I.P. Baskerville
by Western Printing Services Ltd, Bristol
First published 1980

PREFACE

Twenty-five years ago, John Masefield, then Poet Laureate and a friend of long standing, wrote to me, 'I hope so much that you will write a book about storytelling, and try to encourage others to do what you have been doing with so much success.'

Here is the book. It is for all who are interested in stories and would like to tell them—librarians, teachers, play group leaders, parents—would-be storytellers everywhere. Although I am writing in the main about telling stories to groups of children or adults, the same principles apply when the audience is of one child in the home.

This is a very personal book, based on my own experience as a storyteller for over forty years. I have told stories to thousands of children in libraries and schools, and talked to adults about storytelling in all kinds of centres and colleges. As guest storyteller in the United States, Canada, Japan and European countries where English is understood, my audiences have included children and adults of many races. There are no frontiers in the world of stories.

Thanks are due to many librarian friends, particularly in Hertfordshire County libraries, who have shared their experience of storytelling with me. A special 'Thank you' to the many, many children and adults who over the years have shared my stories and made the telling of them such a happy experience. And, of course, my thanks to my editor who has helped me so much with her advice and encouragement.

STORY HOUR

I stood with them before a guarded door,
A door to which I held the magic key.
And all their lifted faces turned to me
As flowers to the sun. And all their words
Were stilled. They waited there to see
What lay beyond the door.

I felt their shy unwillingness to show
Their great desire; and their faith in me,
Their power, their need, their quickened energy
To seize and make their own this shining Hour,
To know the wonder and the mystery
That lay beyond the door.

The silence grew. The sun came in and lay
Across the floor. And then, I think, they knew
The time had come. Slowly the silence grew
Breathless. I moved and slipped the magic key
Into the lock. It turned and—breathless, too—
I opened—wide—the door.

We saw the gleaming towers of Fairyland,
The hills, the rivers, and the arching sky,
The fields and meadows and the lakes that lie
Under the shadows of the whispering trees.
There where the never-ending Road runs by
That leads beyond the door.

We heard the sound of Roland's silver horn
And the clear pipes of Pan among the green.
Here where we pushed aside the leafy screen,
Puck laughed aloud. Then from the hills a band
Of elves and gnomes and fairies swept between
Us and the open door.

The wonder grew. We saw the Table Round,
And—far away—the faint, mysterious flame
Where Fafnir guards the Glittering Hoard. Again
Puck laughed. And kings and emperors stood
And told us tales. All history came
Between us and the door.

And when the Hour was done and we came back
We locked the door again. Yes, but the key
Hangs there within the reach of all. They see
The winding road. They hear the haunting call.
The power is theirs—to know the mystery
That lies beyond the door.

Mary Gould Davis, 1915
(Reprinted by kind permission of *The Horn Book Magazine*)

For more than thirty years Mary Gould Davis told stories in
the New York Public Library. This poem, written early in
her career, was found amongst her papers after her death.

I

What is Storytelling?

'I would not for any quantity of gold part with
the wonderful tales I have retained since my
childhood.'   *Martin Luther*

The love of stories is universal. However different children
are in character and ability, they need stories and love
listening to them. For generations, parents have been familiar with the insistent cry: 'Tell me a story!' Adults, too, given
the opportunity, love stories as much as children. It is no
accident that the greater proportion of books borrowed from
libraries—by both children and adults—are stories of one sort
or another, and that hosts of people watch television simply
for the sake of finding out 'what happens next'.

I have told stories to hundreds of children of all ages, to
laughing West Indian children in the United States, to
immigrants from many nations in Toronto. I have seen four
hundred nuns in a gloomy London hall rocking with laughter at a funny story and a group of refugee women from
Central Europe smiling through tears at a story they had
heard as children in their own country. Students and
teachers, children and parents, all are united by the experience of listening to a story together. You have only to watch
one child—or fifty—listening to a well-told story to realise
how much pleasure stories can give. It is sad that in modern
life there are so many rival demands on the leisure of
adults—and children too—that there seems little time to sit
and tell tales as our ancestors did. But there is always time to
do what we really *want* to do.

Why *tell* a story? Why not read it? There is a place for both
ways of communicating stories, but there is an enormous

difference between the two, both for the adult involved and the child listening. The reader must always be conscious of the printed page before him and can only occasionally look at the audience, while the teller is free to speak directly to them and to watch their reactions. For the child the voice and personality of the storyteller add richness and vitality to the story. The occasion takes on an immediacy and becomes a personal experience for both sides, and an intimate relationship between child and storyteller is established.

Storytelling is made up of three essential elements, the story, the storyteller and the audience. Storytelling cannot be a success unless there is harmony between these three. Given this, there is mutual enjoyment.

First of all, the story, that is, a narrative, usually short enough to be told in one session, of real or fictitious happenings. The variety of stories available to the modern storyteller is infinite. Stories have been told all over the world in every age since man first became articulate. No country is too remote or primitive to possess stories in its own tradition, although they may never have been written down. Stories tell of everyday life, the world of nature, the supernatural, magical and fantastic; they inspire laughter and tears, bring home the virtues of courage, kindness and loyalty, compassion and wonder; portray the ever-present struggle between good and evil; touch the depths of human and spiritual experience.

To link the story and the audience, there must be a storyteller. There is no infallible recipe for the making of a storyteller, for the potential is in everyone. Even the least eloquent of beings can give a convincing account of his or her own personal experiences. This is simply because your own experiences are of absorbing interest to you, so you feel deeply about them and want to talk about them to others. It is easy to describe what has happened to you because you remember it in detail and can *see* it as you put it into words. Here are the essentials for successful storytelling—interest in what you are describing and involvement in the story, a detailed visual picture of its events and a desire that the listener should understand and share your feelings.

Some rare individuals are natural storytellers and are able to tell stories with ease and confidence. Most people, however, are unsure of their ability while others are even convinced that storytelling is totally beyond their capabilities. This is a fallacy, for anyone who is willing to spend some time in study and practice can become a good storyteller. As in life, you can only learn by trial and error, and encouragement is vital if you are to gain confidence. Storytelling is caught rather than taught.

However, certain qualities are naturally an advantage for the would-be storyteller. A creative imagination can give life and colour to a story; a feeling for drama and a degree of skill in portraying character will lend the life and excitement that children so much enjoy. A capacity for seeing the funny side of life on difficult occasions, the humility to laugh at your own affectations, a readiness to share the children's rather slapstick sense of humour, all help enormously. Similarly, a storyteller should have the grace to acknowledge a wrong choice of story, insufficient preparation, a dullness in presentation—these are the storyteller's fault, and cannot be blamed on some strange lack of sensitivity in the audience. A wide knowledge of books of all kinds is invaluable, and its corollary, a good vocabulary, ensures command of the most effective words and a liveliness in telling. Above all, you must believe in the value of telling stories to children, or the necessary preparation will be without heart or purpose.

Through the medium of storytelling children are introduced to ideas, emotions and thoughts in a way they can understand and which gives them enjoyment, wonder and fun. Although children may learn a great deal as they listen, this is not the primary reason for telling stories. Stories provide a stimulus to the imagination which cannot be found elsewhere. That 'the world has widened and the imagination of man has dwindled' is perhaps true. The child's imagina-

3

tion must be stimulated from an early age if he is to develop as a person. Without it he is locked into a narrow environment bounded by what he is able to see and touch. With imagination he has a key to open 'magic casements' into a world of richness and colour where anything can happen. Imagination enables him to see a landscape he has never seen, to take part in adventures he may never experience, to share in other people's lives and so develop compassion and understanding for different ways of living. But imagination needs food and stimulus and here the rhymes and stories the child hears when young are invaluable. How young? This varies with the individual, but certainly long before he goes to school. Some parents claim that the process can begin at eighteen months and certainly by the age of two. This largely depends on the adults in a child's life, for it is their responsibility to introduce picture books, stories and rhymes to children.

How many generations of children have listened entranced as some storyteller began 'Once upon a time. . .'! The response of children to storytelling is shown by complete absorption in the story, a feeling of anticipation or sadness according to the mood of the story and a satisfied sigh as it ends in the time-honoured formula: 'And they lived happily ever after.'

These responses are tangible, but there are others which we may never realise. The storyteller may think the story will soon be forgotten, but for the child it may become a treasured memory for years to come. I have told stories long enough to have had the experience of hearing an adult, once a child in one of my storytelling sessions, say, 'Do you remember that story you used to tell us as children? I have never forgotten it. Now I am sharing it with my own children.'

Through listening to stories the child becomes aware of the magic and music of words, and if the storyteller chooses wisely, her stories will awaken an appreciation of the great stories and traditional tales which are the heritage of every child. Storytelling helps to restore the importance of the spoken word at a time when the emphasis is on the visual, when the heroes of television and film often take the place of the mysterious figures of fairy tales and mythology in the child's world. Children are now less willing and able to listen without the aid of visual images. While it is quite common to hear stories read or watch them dramatised, one rarely has the opportunity to hear a story told spontaneously. I believe that television can never be more than a substitute for the living story told by an adult who is close to the child.

When storyteller and child meet, life is enriched for both by the sharing of a story. To have laughed together, shared excitement or sadness, experienced wonder and emotion, establishes a mutual feeling of warmth and comradeship, an experience worth all that it may cost in time and energy.

2

Storytelling—

Then and Now

'. . . a tale which holdeth children from play
and old men from the chimney corner.'
Sir Philip Sidney

The storyteller of today is a link in the long chain of storytellers stretching into the past and future. Before the days of
writing, when the spoken word was the only means of com-
munication, stories were an essential and enjoyable part of
life. Without written records, the history and laws of a tribe
had to be remembered and passed on orally, often in the
form of stories. Through stories truths and patterns of
behaviour can be conveyed and are more easily understood
and remembered. The give-and-take between storyteller
and audience has always been a vital educational experience
and provides a stimulus for speech and self-expression. From
the early days, storytelling had an importance and value for
everyone in the community.

Two of the most common types of stories in the earliest
days of storytelling were very likely what Arthur Ransome
called the 'Warning Example' and the 'Embroidered
Exploit'. Mothers of every generation have known the necessity and effectiveness of warning children against danger by
an example in the form of a story. 'Once there was a child',
says the mother, 'who *would* go down to the river although his
mother told him not to. Listen to what happened to him. . .'
Such warning stories would often be aimed not only at
children but at any member of the community who offended

against the laws of the tribe. The 'Embroidered Exploit' would have originated as a factual report of a hunter's encounter with some wild animal, for example. Exaggeration was inevitable with each retelling, so that in course of time the exploit assumed such magnitude that it was far beyond the capabilities of any human being. Thus the story became one of extraordinary feats by some supernatural being.

Stories also developed as a means of explaining natural phenomena, such as thunder and lightning, earthquakes and floods, and the changing seasons. Inevitably such stories involved supernatural beings: in Norse mythology, Thor beat out thunder with his hammer, and in the Greek myths Ceres' distress over the rape of her daughter Persephone could cause drought and disrupt the seasons. Man's ignorance of natural causes resulted in a wealth of imaginative tales.

Tolkien likens 'Story' to a pot of soup into which almost everything has been dropped—scraps of history, religion, legends, dreams, magic and magical objects—and out of which almost anything can come. It is certain, however, that stories have always been travellers, carried by Roman legionnaires, pilgrims, crusaders, sailors, gypsies, and exchanged with others from many lands. In all centuries, not least our own, there have been refugees fleeing from invading armies, who have forgotten their loneliness for a time as they told the stories of their homeland.

At first every man was his own storyteller, but inevitably one member of the tribe would stand out for his skill and effectiveness in relating his own and his fellows' tales. As time went on, such men would devote all their lives to remembering and telling the tribal stories of past history and heroic deeds.

These early professional storytellers established a traditional custom which was to endure in many forms and in many lands for centuries. At this time storytellers usually sang or chanted their stories, perhaps in simple verse forms, to the music of a primitive, harp-like instrument. They had many names—in northern lands, in what is now known as Scandinavia, storytellers were known as Scalds. They rode with the king into battle so that they might sing of his valour and they occupied a privileged position in his retinue: they could expect to receive a harp from the king and a ring from the queen and to be ransomed if captured in war. In Wales the storytellers were called Bards and had apprentices known as Maninogs. To become a Master Bard, the apprentice had to learn a great number of stories from his Master. These were handed down from generation to generation by word of mouth. In Ireland the storytellers were known as Ollamhs or Seanachies. Each one could recite two hundred tales—one eighth-century storyteller told a different tale each night from Samain to Beltane (November 1st to May 1st)!

There have been storytellers in England for many centuries. In the fourth century a 'gleeman' named Widsith sang and said a story in the mead hall and was given a collar of beaten gold and a ring in return. Bede relied considerably on 'the traditions of our forefathers'—stories and poems handed down orally for centuries—in his *Ecclesiastical History of the English People*. Caedmon of Whitby composed not only sacred poems but secular rhymes for gleemen to sing.

With the coming of the Normans the Saxon gleemen almost disappeared. They could not compete with the more sophisticated Norman minstrels, especially as the language of the Court was now French. These storytellers were welcome everywhere, for they were often the only means of entertainment in the long winter evenings. Storytelling was an accepted part of daily life and in the draughty baronial halls of castles, the lord, his family, servants and men-at-arms would gather round the fire to listen to tales told by some traveller or minstrel. Whether it was a manor house or a peasant's thatched dwelling, someone would tell a story to keep the darkness and its perils away. It was considered only common politeness to repay hospitality with a story. 'England was conquered to the music of verse and settled to the sound of the harp', says the historian Stopford Brooke.

The minstrel was a colourful figure. Dressed in unusual, brightly coloured clothes, his instrument at hand, he wandered about the country, visiting castle, manor house or market place, reciting the old tales, sometimes in verse, sometimes in prose, of *Bevis of Southampton*, *Beowulf*, *Guy of Warwick* and many others. Sometimes he had a retinue which included a buffoon to make people laugh, a tumbler (juggler) and a musician. Minstrels were present at every important occasion, and had a great deal of influence, for they could win the ear of the people and weave complaints against the unpopular taxes or public figures into their stories and songs. Edward I, for example, had many in his train, including two women, Matill Makejoye and Pearl in the Egg.

Storytelling was by no means confined to these specialists, but was a familiar feature of everyday life until the fifteenth century. As we know from *The Canterbury Tales*, on every pilgrimage travellers told stories to while away the tedious journey. Everywhere, sermons were usually illustrated by stories until the religious reformer, Wycliffe, and other churchmen denounced the custom on the grounds that such tales kept alive pagan beliefs.

The invention of printing in the fifteenth century gradually brought to an end the telling of tales by professional minstrels whose public had been found mainly in the homes of the richer members of the community. With the foundation of schools and the spread of education, many people amongst the upper and merchant classes were able to read for themselves. For the people in the market place, ballad singers who recited or sang popular verses about topical events or the deeds of folk heroes took the place of minstrels. But the same stories survived in various forms. Amongst the first of Caxton's printed works were Malory's *Morte d'Arthur*, which was based on old French and Celtic tales of romance kept alive by minstrels for generations, and *Reynard the Fox*.

For centuries more, however, the tradition of storytelling lingered among the ordinary people in town and country. Stories were passed on by word of mouth, usually by the older men and women to the family or small gatherings of neighbours. In the *Anatomy of Melancholy*, written in the sixteenth century, Robert Burton claims that the ordinary recreations of people in winter were 'merry tales of errant knights, queens, lovers, lords, ladies, giants, dwarfs, thieves, cheaters, witches, fayries, goblins . . . which some delight to hear, some to tell, and all are well pleased with.' The traditional material passed down orally consisted largely of fairy and folk tales, romances and hero stories.

By degrees the custom of telling tales as an accepted part of everyday life disappeared. Why was this? One theory is that it declined because of the altered rhythm of life which came with the Industrial Revolution and the invention of better lighting for the home. No longer did men and women carry on their traditional working skills at home in the evenings while someone told a story. Now the men, and often the women and children too, worked in factories for long hours. The brighter lights, the weariness of the people and the sheer lack of leisure time, were not conducive to the telling of tales. Newspapers and books quickly took over from the storyteller's memory. The oral tradition was dying out and by the nineteenth century learned men were collecting the old stories as folklore rather than as something living to share and enjoy.

Although storytelling was no longer part of daily life in towns by the nineteenth century, it still lingered in remote parts of the countryside. These rural storytellers could recite many tales of heroic quests, exploits and legendary history. A collector of folk tales recorded no less than 375 tales from Peig Sayers, a storyteller of Gaelic tales who lived all her life on the bleak Great Basket Island off the coast of Kerry. She was known as 'The Queen of Gaelic storytellers' and died as recently as 1958. In the introduction to her book, *An Old Woman's Reflections*, she describes a typical storytelling:

> In a whitewashed kitchen in the glen the peat-fire glows like a berry, and the cricket—'the cock of the ashes'—sings. And the tangle of Gaelic voices singles out as the Storyteller spreads his fingers for attention and begins his tale.

Only recently an old Irishman told me that his most vivid childhood memory was of listening to an Irish Seanachie, a Gaelic teller of legendary romances, telling stories in a cottage within the sound of the sea.

Storytelling is still a living tradition in many countries where education and books are not readily available. In Morocco storytellers are found in market places and in Egypt Bedouins listen to professional storytellers with loud clapping of hands. In Java the honoured 'Dalang' chants tales from the *Ramayana*, moving puppets against a screen. In Nigeria villagers welcome travelling storytellers whose tales have an important part to play in educating children in tribal customs and tradition. Similarly the Aborigines of Australia pass on the beliefs and folklore of their ancestors by word of mouth. Written words are often only a substitute for our need to have beauty and terror and laughter brought to us by the human voice.

In the western world the art of storytelling has declined, although there are some signs of a revival of interest, particularly in the United States and Australia. In the United States the interest in storytelling, fostered by librarians, has spread through the organisation of storytelling workshops during which students listen to stories and are taught how to tell them. Occasionally a festival is held, a day or week set apart for listening to and telling stories for pleasure. In New England, for instance, there is such a festival held annually in memory of two outstanding storytellers, Alice Jordan and Bertha Mahoney Miller.

Britain has many storytellers whose names may only be

known locally but who keep the art alive and share stories with children. In 1922, an English teacher, Marie Shedlock, travelled through war-torn France telling stories to the children of devastated areas in their own language. She was a wonderful interpreter of Andersen's stories and practised her art in both America and England. Better known here is the name of Elizabeth Clark, an inspired storyteller who gave demonstrations to colleges of education, libraries and universities. I still come across teachers who remember the way this unassuming woman could entrance large gatherings of students. Elizabeth Clark's collections of stories retold from folk tales, legends and literature are still excellent material. All her stories were tested with children before being included in her books.

Whatever the origin of stories, the same basic patterns appear again and again round the world, passing from mouth to mouth and from generation to generation for centuries and giving pleasure to countless hearers. For example, 'Nix Nought Nothing', one of those stories in which a father, unaware of his son's birth, promises to give 'Nix Nought Nothing' to an enemy in order to save his own life, is found in India, Egypt, Greece, Zululand, North and South America, Samoa, Russia and Africa. 'Puss-in-Boots' originated in Arabia, travelled to Italy and France, then to Scandinavia, Africa, the East, and Russia. Joseph Jacobs once said that he had edited an English version of an Italian adaptation of a Spanish translation of a Latin version of a Hebrew translation of an Arabic translation of an Indian original. Names and background may alter but basic plots remain. And behind all these ancient tales and before all written literature, is the voice of the anonymous storyteller.

3

What Shall I Tell?

Stories for pre-school children

Perhaps the hardest part of storytelling is selecting a story, not because of a shortage of material but because there is so much to choose from. Yet selection is also a most interesting and rewarding exercise. In looking for a story to tell, you will extend your knowledge and appreciation of literature of all kinds, discovering new and challenging byways, learning discrimination as you select.

Choosing a story is always a very personal matter, for unless it appeals to you, it is difficult to tell with enthusiasm and conviction. I have seen would-be storytellers try to tell a story which they had chosen as suitable in theory but which they did not themselves enjoy. The result is inevitably disastrous. If you really like a story and are eager to share it, you will be halfway to success. Without this qualification, the audience is likely to be apathetic or restless simply because they do not believe in the story.

An important point to remember when selecting stories is that the appeal to the eye is different from that to the ear. Some stories are for reading, some for telling. The structure of the story as a whole, the length of the sentences, the general pattern, is different in the two kinds of story. Consider, for instance, two such widely differing stories as Andersen's 'The Little Mermaid' and Wanda Gag's *Gone is Gone*, a version of the folk tale of the man who thought he could keep house better than his wife. Andersen's story opens with a long description of the world under the sea where the mermaids live and it is only on the sixth page that the Little Mermaid attains her desire to see 'the upper world'. In *Gone is Gone* the story begins at once with a minimum of description:

> This man, his name was Fritz—his wife, her name was Liesi. They had a little baby, Kinndli by name, and Spitz who was a dog.

The Little Mermaid's story is told in long sentences and paragraphs, using a wide vocabulary and poetic images. In Wanda Gag's story, sentences are short, the vocabulary familiar and domestic and the plot uncomplicated, so that the story is easy to comprehend at the first hearing. The emphasis in Andersen is on the emotions so that the story moves slowly and needs to be read thoughtfully as a moving and imaginative experience. *Gone is Gone* moves quickly from one amusing incident to the next until the expected climax when Liesi comes home to find chaos. The title phrase, repeated many times, invites children to join in, and there is a feeling of spontaneity, the mark of a story that has been told by many storytellers. It is obvious that here is a story to be *told*—and equally obvious that 'The Little Mermaid' needs to be read alone so that its beauty, pathos and underlying meaning can be fully appreciated and lingered over. With experience the storyteller learns to distinguish almost instinctively between a story for telling and a story for reading. The beginner should look out for these characteristics: direct colloquial speech which establishes a relationship between teller and audience, a minimum of description and plenty of action.

The way in which a story is written can add beauty and life to what would otherwise be rather ordinary material. The individual way in which an author handles words, his or her powers of expressing emotion, of giving life to a character, of evoking a landscape—all these have a part to play in building up an author's style. Take the old fairy tale, 'The Sleeping Beauty' in Arthur Rackham's *Fairy Book*. The princess has just pricked her finger with the spindle:

. . . Though it was but a small wound, she immediately fainted and fell to the floor . . . There she lay, as beautiful as an angel, with the colour still lingering in her lips and cheeks, but her eyes were tightly closed. . .

Here is Walter de la Mare's description of the same incident, from *Tales Told Again:*

Before even the blood had welled up to the size of a bead upon her thumb, the wicked magic of the Fairy began to enter into her body. Slowly, drowsily, the princess' eyelids began to descend over her dark blue eyes; her two hands slid softly down on either side of her; her head drooped lower and lower towards her pillow. She put out her two hands, as if groping her way; sighed; sank lower; and soon she had fallen fast, fast asleep.

Note how evocative and musical this passage is—and almost soporific in its effect! The stories a child hears can enrich his vocabulary and train his ear to respond to the music and rhythm of words. And children can certainly appreciate these qualities. A child of nine wrote this about words:

> The boring words—
> I look at them dragging their feet.
> But when the exciting marvellous words
> Jump out, I dance and sing with them.
> The boring, dreary words
> Slip back into the book.
> Good luck to them!
> I like the words
> Which liven me up.

Every story needs time and energy in its preparation so it is never worth choosing one which you feel is trivial or commonplace. Such stories can only give momentary pleasure rather than an imaginative experience. The vulgar, the cynical, the sadistic, have no place in stories for children, widespread as they are in everyday life; the emphasis must surely be on qualities worthy of emulation—loyalty, courage and kindness.

Obviously it is important to take the audience into account when choosing a story to tell. It may be of boys or girls or both, of children from homes where books are an accepted way of life, or from a neighbourhood where children do not hear stories in the home, or indeed, see books at all. The age of the children in the audience will influence your choice, which is largely a matter of common sense. Obviously if you tell a fairy story to boys of thirteen or read from *Hamlet* to an audience of infants, as I once heard an eminent actor do, you must accept the consequences! The problem arises when the storyteller is faced, perhaps unexpectedly, with a group of mixed age-range, say six-to-ten-year-olds. Shall we choose a story for the older children or the younger? I have found that there are many stories which can be enjoyed by a wide age-range, usually folk stories. 'The Magic Umbrella' by Rose Fyleman, the Japanese tale of 'The Magic Kettle' by Rhoda Power, 'Two of Everything' by Alice Ritchie, are all successful with a varied age-group. All these stories are amusing, and can be told simply so that the younger children can understand them. The Russian tale 'Volkh's Journey to the East' by E. M. Almedingen, is an adventure story which has great appeal, for each child can keep count of the number of wishes the young hero has left, and the suspense of the situation holds the attention of all ages. I have found also on numerous occasions that if I appeal to the older members of the group to wait patiently while I tell a story to the younger ones, they will do so. Incidentally, they are then free to enjoy a younger story without embarrassment while at the same time feeling virtuous and kindly! Whatever their age, each child takes from the story what he is *ready* to appreciate at his stage of development.

It is important to treat children as sensible beings and as equals. Even a hint of condescension not only causes resentment but is unfair to the child and creates a gap between him and the adult. Whatever the age-group it is wise to choose a story which will lead children a stage further on in their development and 'stretch and stimulate their little minds', as Dr Johnson said. Most children look forward with touching optimism to the day when they will be grown-up,and no child likes to be treated as an inferior being incapable of understanding a story which seems to be a little beyond his understanding or reading ability. In fact, most children can understand much more when listening to a story than when reading it alone.

Sometimes storytelling is an impromptu affair for the storyteller, snatched from a busy period because a small group of restless children offers an opportunity for the introduction of a story. For such occasions no plan can be made in advance other than ensuring that you have a good stock of stories to draw upon. For the more formal occasions in library or school, some kind of programme is advisable if the best possible use is to be made of the time available. In schools there is usually a set time for stories, the age-group is constant and the mental age of the children is also known, so that it is easier to choose suitable stories. In libraries stories must be told at a regular time which will fit into the schedule of opening hours and staff duties. Attendance is voluntary and audiences cannot always be divided into age-groups, so are likely to be of mixed ages. The storyteller may know some of the children, but by no means all. It is harder therefore to plan a programme in advance but advisable to do so all the same.

In this chapter the kind of stories most suitable for children of pre-school age is discussed. Children of five to twelve will be dealt with in the next chapter.

Pre-school children are found in playgroups, nursery schools, libraries and, of course, at home. For children as young as this the programme must not last more than half an hour, for the span of attention of three-to-five-year-olds is short and they are too full of energy to sit still and listen for a longer period. In fact even a half-hour session should be broken up with a more active interlude.

In playgroups it is often difficult to persuade children to leave their activities and games to hear a story. It must be proved by its presentation that storytime can be a pleasurable part of the day and that it has something interesting and exciting to offer. Once this has been established, children can look forward to this quieter period. Incidentally, the opportunity it provides to *look* and *listen* is invaluable to a child's development at this early stage.

The main source of stories for young children are picture books and collections of simple tales like those found in the Young Puffin series. Children love stories of pets, home life, shopping with mother, walks in the park—the everyday life they know. Stories in which machines, cars and planes have human characteristics—such as Diana Ross' *The Little Red Engine* or Val Biro's *Gumdrop* (a vintage car)—are usually particular favourites.

It is advisable to break up the storytime for young children into three parts—a picture book, an interval of participation and a second story. First the picture book. Physically the book must be large enough for all the group to see—fifteen or twenty children at one time is the limit. It follows that the ubiquitous paperback is not practical for this purpose, although it is satisfactory for a child to hold and look at closely on his own. Pictures should be bold, clear and brightly coloured. Hold the book facing the children at a suitable height and turn the pages slowly as you tell the story, allowing time for your audience to absorb each picture and relate it to the words.

The text of a picture book to be shown in such a way must be simple and direct:

> Once upon a time there were three little kittens, and their names were Mittens, Tom Kitten and Moppet. . .

or this from Judith Kerr's *The Tiger who came to tea:*

Sophie opened the door, and there was a big, furry, stripy tiger. The tiger said, 'Excuse me, but I'm very hungry. Do you think I could have tea with you?' Sophie's Mummy said, 'Of course, come in.'

Repetition in words or pictures is essential. Pat Hutchins' *Rosie's Walk* is a brilliant example, with its repetitive pictures showing Rosie the hen strutting across page after page, supremely unconscious of her danger from the pursuing fox. In *The Elephant and the Bad Baby* by Elfrida Vipont and Raymond Briggs, the Elephant and the Bad Baby go 'rumpeta, rumpeta, all down the road,' a phrase which is repeated time after time to the pleasurable anticipation of the children. The sound of words can seem very funny to children and invented names of the 'ploshy-sloshy' type can usually be relied upon to excite chuckles.

However simple the story, something must happen in the text and pictures. Beautiful, abstract paintings and drawings can never have the universal appeal of a good story told in pictures and words, and illustrations must always be representational enough for the child to recognise. Perennial favourites are the 'Babar' stories, 'Mr Gumpy' and *Harry the Dirty Dog*.

After the picture-book story, it is time for a change to something a little more active which will involve the child. This is when finger plays—rhymes accompanied by movements of the fingers and hands—are useful, not only because they demand participation, but because they also help the child to co-ordinate the movements of his hands in various actions. Watch a young child and you will realise how difficult this can be! Take a very simple example of a finger play: 'A little mouse hid in a hole' (place the first finger of the left hand between thumb and finger of the closed fist of the right hand). 'Hid softly in a little hole. When all was quiet as quiet could be' (at this point every child is still, eyes fixed on the leader's hands. Pause for a second or two then withdraw the left-hand finger quickly) 'OUT POPPED HE!' 'I was first!' cries a child. 'I was firster!' shouts another. After a few repetitions, every child is joining in and laughing with excitement. Finger plays are simple games which involve every child both physically and mentally and as such have a great value. A great variety of such rhymes to use from babyhood onwards is to be found in Norah Montgomerie's *This Little Pig Went to Market* and Elizabeth Matterson's paperback *This Little Puffin*. The latter includes action songs and musical games for more active occasions. The words of these rhymes suggest the actions and the storyteller can easily invent new variations.

Nursery rhymes are also good material for the pre-school storytime interval. Today nursery rhymes are often neglected and many children know only two or three because this is all their parents readily remember. Nursery rhymes are important, for they are the child's first introduction to a simple form of poetry, rhyme and rhythm. They have survived — some of them for centuries — because their form and the pictures they evoke make them easy to remember. 'Little Boy Blue', 'Baa baa, black sheep' and the charming 'I had a little nut tree' are good examples. At this stage of their development, children learn easily through repetition and enjoy chanting or singing nursery rhymes. If actions can be fitted to the words, so much the better, as this makes them still easier to remember. 'Sing a song of sixpence' is a favourite for this reason. It has many actable lines: 'The Queen was in the parlour, Eating bread and honey . . . down came a blackbird and pecked off her nose . . .' (Some children need reassurance about this!) Useful collections of nursery rhymes are Nicola Bayley's, illustrated by beautiful, detailed full colour paintings, and Iona and Peter Opie's *Puffin Book of Nursery Rhymes*.

Occasionally the interval can be more active, with the children marching round the room to the tune of 'The Grand Old Duke of York' or playing some simple game like 'Here we come gathering nuts and may'. But this takes up time, and it can be difficult to recapture the children's attention afterwards. It is best to save such activities for special occasions, to create a party atmosphere at Christmas or before the summer break.

After the interval, the children, relaxed, will be ready to listen to the second and last story. This can be *without* pictures, provided it is uncomplicated, brief and concerned with familiar things which the child can visualise for himself. The well-loved traditional tale 'The Three Bears' is a good one to use and there are many collections of other suitable stories. For instance, *Playtime Stories* by Joyce Donoghue, tales of young children in their own homes; my own collections, *The Youngest Storybook*, *Tell Me a Story* and their successors; the 'Ponder and William' stories by Barbara Softly; the 'Milly-Molly-Mandy' stories by Joyce L. Brisley, old-fashioned perhaps, but still enjoyed by children for their homeliness. Children love to laugh, so look out for funny stories like *Mrs Pepperpot* or Donald Bisset's *The Quacking Pillarbox*.

This pattern of programme—picture-book story, an interval of finger plays and a second story—answers well for a group of pre-school children. On the following page there is a suggested programme as a guide, but there can be infinite variations according to the taste of the storyteller and the books available.

Pre-School Storytime

Lively tune on tape-recorder as children come in. Don't forget to ask if any child has a birthday.

PROGRAMME

PICTURE BOOKS	*Wild Animals* Brian Wildsmith
	The Hungry Caterpillar Eric Carle
INTERVAL	
Finger Plays	'A little Mouse hid in a hole. . .'
	'Here is a tree with leaves so green'
	'Five currant buns in a baker's shop'
	(From *This Little Puffin*)
Nursery Rhymes	'Baa, baa, black sheep'
	(learnt the previous week)
	'Ride a cock-horse. . .'
STORY WITHOUT	'The Dog that Had No Name'
PICTURES	Leila Berg (From *Time for a Story*
	Eileen Colwell)
CLOSING RHYME	'Two little hands go clap, clap, clap.
	Two little feet go tap, tap, tap.
	Two little arms high in the air,
	ONE BIG JUMP UP FROM
	THE CHAIR!'

4

What Shall I Tell?

Stories for five-to-twelve-year-olds

'What shall we tell you? Tales, marvellous tales
Of ships and stars and isles where good men
  rest,
Where nevermore the rose of summer pales,
And winds and shadows fall towards the West.'
                    (*The Golden Journey to Samarkand*)
                    James Elroy Flecker

This chapter will deal with two age-groups, the five-to-
seven-year-olds and the eight-to-twelve-year-olds. Both
groups enjoy the same kinds of stories—folk tales and fantasy, hero tales, adventure, stories about animals and funny
stories. Inevitably the two groups overlap, for they are composed of individuals who can vary greatly in their powers of
comprehension and appreciation. It is not wise, therefore, to
say dogmatically that a particular story will not appeal to
children because of their age. What decides the children's
reaction to a story is the way in which it is presented and this
is largely a matter of experience. A story you might think of
using with an older group can often be told more simply for a
younger group while remaining basically the same. However, it is usually a question of choosing stories which are
younger in content—Robin Hood rather than King Arthur,
Ursula Moray Williams' *The Good Little Christmas Tree*
(which has the feeling of a fairy tale and includes much

23

repetition) rather than the Breton legend, 'Brother Johan-nick and his Silver Bell' (which is more mature and has a religious background). Alison Uttley's tales of magic and enchantment are suitable for older children, while her 'Sam Pig' and 'Tim Rabbit' stories appeal to the younger ones.

It should be remembered that the fives-to-sevens include children who, not so long ago, had their first experience of school. When a young.child first goes to school, his taste and appreciation of stories begins to widen. Gradually his span of attention lengthens and his comprehension develops. He has new-found interests and confidence, yet at the same time finds reassurance in hearing familiar stories he associates with infancy. While he still enjoys 'The Three Bears' and other nursery tales, he can now appreciate a longer and more robust story from Grimm, or Andersen's 'The Tinder Box' for example. He still enjoys a picture book but it must have a longer, more mature text. Charles Keeping's *Charley, Charlotte and the Golden Canary*, the story of two friends who are separated by the demolition of their homes and find each other again through a 'golden' canary, or Edward Ardiz-zone's 'Tim' stories, are both suitable choices.

These younger children appreciate a simple ceremony to begin their story-session. I would recommend something along the lines of that used in the New York Library. A candle is lit as a sign that the story is about to begin and at the end of the session the youngest child blows it out and all make a secret wish. It is a good idea to begin with a picture book, followed by a story without pictures, such as Paul Beigel's *The King of the Copper Mountains*, in which a beloved old king is kept alive by his interest in the intriguing stories told by his friends, the animals, until a magic herb can be brought to cure him. In between the stories there is time for a poem or two from Robert Louis Stevenson's *A Child's Garden of Verses* or Barbara Ireson's *Rhyme Time*. Half an hour is long enough for this younger age-group.

An opening ceremony is unnecessary for the eights-totwelves, but it is a good idea to welcome newcomers in a friendly way. A group of children of this age offers an opportunity to tell a wide variety of stories, particularly if it meets regularly over a period of time. A season of stories can have a theme to help with continuity—animal stories, hero tales, tales of magic or folk tales from different cultures represented in the group. A thirty-to-forty minute storytime for this age-group might include a Greek legend, 'The Gorgon's Head', a French-Canadian story, 'The Golden Phoenix' by Marius Barbeau, and, as an extra to laugh at, Richard Hughes' 'The Elephant's Picnic'. In between the stories try introducing a poem. You will find plenty of suitable examples in *Figgie Hobbin*, Charles Causley's hilarious, moving collection, or in Leila Berg's selection of poetry about animals, *Four Feet and Two*. Poems by Ian Serraillier, Eleanor Farjeon and James Reeves are all popular.

Now to consider in more detail the varied kinds of stories suitable for the two age-groups.

Of all the kinds of stories told by storytellers, the fairy tale is the richest source. What do we mean by fairy stories? Not just 'them made-up things . . . little buzzflies with butterfly wings and gauze petticoats, and shiny stars in their hair'—we would agree with Kipling's Puck that the day for these is past. Modern children prefer more robust material but they still enjoy stories of magic with fairy-tale patterns, as a recent 'Jackanory' story-writing competition proved—of the six thousand entries, the largest proportion had fairy-tale themes. For the storyteller, Tolkien's definition of fairy stories, in his essay 'Tree and Leaf', is the most satisfying:

Faerie, the realm or state in which fairies have their being, contains many things besides dwarfs, witches, trolls, giants, or dragons: it holds the seas, the sun, the moon, the sky; and the earth, and all things that are in it: tree and bird, water and stone, wine and bread, and ourselves, mortal men, when we are enchanted. . .

Psychologists say that fairy tales are necessary to a child's development and give form and substance to his imaginings. In them he finds vicarious adventure, danger and conflict, joy and sorrow, good and evil, life and death. These basic and constant patterns appeal to the insecure child who knows that the third and weakest son will triumph; the dragon or the loathly monster will always be destroyed, the good be victorious.

Fairy tales have all the components of ideal stories for telling; they are direct, there is plenty of action, the instruments of magic are homely, the settings are natural—mountains, forests, rivers and lakes. There are several distinct types of fairy tales for the storyteller to choose from. For five-to-seven-year-olds there are 'cumulative tales' such as 'The Old Woman and her Pig' or 'Henny-Penny'. For seven-to-ten-year-olds, there are the 'Drolls', down-to-earth stories of simple people typified by the world-famous tale 'The Man who Thought he Could Keep House Better than his Wife' (Wanda Gág's version *Gone is Gone*, is very effective for telling), or 'The Three Sillies' which, with its repetitive phrase and ridiculous situations inevitably excites spontaneous laughter.

For most children, tales of magic are the favourites, from 'Cinderella', that ancient tale of which there are so many variants, to the homely 'The Elves and the Shoemaker'. Witches are always popular for they give half-fearful pleasure, and can be overcome by brave and clever children like the 'little girl with a kind heart' in Arthur Ransome's 'Baba Yaga'. Today there are many tales of 'good' witches, but to children the only good witch is a bad one! Good witches—or dragons—are disappointing, for children enjoy naughty children and villains in stories as a vicarious substitute for their own forbidden naughtiness. Hence the popularity of Christianna Brand's *Nurse Matilda* and my own *Bad Boys*.

Talking animals figure largely in children's traditional stories—'The Three Billy-goats Gruff', and 'The Three Pigs' for the younger children, the 'Brer Rabbit' stories or the West Indian 'Annancy' tales (and many, many more), for the older children. A good source is Kathleen Arnott's *Animal Folk Tales Around the World*.

The number of collections of fairy stories available today is enormous. Almost every country in the world is represented, each with its national characteristics but often with similar basic themes. Collections of this kind can be found in abundance on library shelves, but every storyteller should own copies of the standard collections—Joseph Jacobs' *English Fairy Tales*, Andersen and Grimm and some version of Perrault—and would find Katharine Briggs' *Abbey Lubbers, Banshees and Boggarts: a Who's Who of Fairies* a fascinating source book.

Illustrated versions of fables provide excellent material for five-to-seven-year-olds. The best-known fables are attributed to Aesop, and La Fontaine included many of these in his classic collection. These brief dramatic stories lend themselves readily to imaginative expansion, for example, 'The Town Mouse and the Country Mouse', 'The Wind and the Sun' and 'The Miller, his Son and their Ass'.

Greek and Roman myths are sadly neglected today, yet without some knowledge of them, many allusions in literature and art are meaningless. The stories of Ceres and Persephone, of Icarus falling through the sky, his wings singed by his daring flight to the sun, of Midas and the Golden Touch or of Bellerophon and the taming of the winged horse, are unforgettable and provide an invaluable stimulus to the imagination. Children may not understand the allegory and symbolism of such tales, but they will certainly be enchanted by the stories themselves. There are many versions of the myths and there can be all kinds of differences in choice of words, complexity, emphasis and angles of approach. Readers who are interested in versions of this and other traditional material, will find a thoughtful and detailed analysis in Elizabeth Cook's *The Ordinary and the Fabulous*. Myths are not suitable for the younger age-group but can well be used with eight-to-ten-year-olds; their imagery and romance often have great appeal for teenagers, too. Do not present them as classical tales of long ago, a school subject for study, but tell them as *stories* to be enjoyed like any other tales for their own sake.

Similarly, it is worth telling the absorbing adventures of Odysseus to ten-to-twelve-year-olds. The stories of his fight with the one-eyed giant Polyphemus, his encounter with the sorceress Circe and with the Sirens, and his dramatic return home to confront his wife's suitors, are exciting and often prove highly popular with this age-group.

The Norse myths are in a more heroic mood. They are concerned with the larger-than-life relationship between the gods of Asgard, men in Midgard, the Giants in Jotunheimen and the 'multitudinous dead' in Niflheim. Gods and men are threatened by the inexorable approach of Ragnarok, day of doom, when all will be destroyed. Stories which appeal to older children are 'The Apples of Iduna', 'How Odin Lost his Eye' and in particular 'The Death of Baldur'. Useful collections are Roger L. Green's *Myths of the Norsemen* and Kevin Crossley-Holland's *The Faber Book of Northern Legends*.

Norse sagas tell of heroic achievements by men who, although beset by gods and men, show immense courage and endurance. Heroism, loyalty, death rather than dishonour, are the principles that rule the lives of these legendary Norsemen and there is a sweep and excitement in the stories about them. The thirteenth-century Icelandic stories of Grettir the Strong, an outlawed hero who suffered many misfortunes and fought his foes courageously, and of Njal, a wise and brave man who, because of a blood feud, tragically lost his life, are both good, stirring adventure stories for older children.

Ireland has always been the land of storytelling and of legendary heroes, the two most famous being Cuchulain and Finn Mac Cool. The legends surrounding them are complex and compassionate, a blend of folklore, hero tales and romance. Many are too violent and full of 'battle frenzy' to offer to children, but both Cuchulain and Finn personify youth and wild courage and as such have great appeal for the over-tens. The so-called 'three sorrows of storytelling' which include the story of 'The Children of Lir', who were changed into swans by their wicked stepmother and condemned to sail the seas for a thousand years, form an introduction to these cycles. Another very popular story is that of 'Oisin the Harpist and Niahm of the Golden Hair' who rode away to Tir-na-Og, the Land of the Ever Young, on a white horse—'and those who watched from the green land saw them no more.'

All children should know something about the legends of King Arthur and his Knights of the Round Table. Because of their complexity and subject matter, their appeal is largely to children of about twelve, although Gwyn Jones' 'Where Arthur Sleeps' is a fine, dramatic tale suitable for eight-to-ten-year-olds. I have found the most popular stories from the cycle to be the drawing of the sword Excalibur, Merlin's spells and the passing of Arthur. There are many good retellings: Roger L. Green's *King Arthur and His Knights of the Round Table* is very useful. It's a good idea to introduce an occasional quotation from Tennyson's *Idylls of the King* to build up the atmosphere. The story of the quest for the Holy Grail is complicated but fortunately there is a beautiful and succinct retelling in Rosemary Sutcliff's *The Light Beyond the Forest*.

There are many other enjoyable hero tales. One favourite is that of the friendship between Roland and Oliver, both Paladins of Charlemagne, whose tragic end at Roncesvalles is told by Ian Serraillier in *The Ivory Horn*. Every country has a national hero around whose exploits legends have gathered, a rich source of stories.

Younger children are fascinated by England's legendary national hero, Robin Hood, helped by the highly romanticised versions on television and in films. Robin Hood's championship of the poor and weak and the tricks he plays on those in authority have won him an enduring place in the affections of children. Most of the stories originally come from ballads but are told by storytellers in prose. A useful collection is Rosemary Sutcliff's *The Chronicles of Robin Hood*. Ballads are close neighbours to hero tales. They tell of heroic deeds and romantic encounters, whether legendary or with some historical basis, from 'Sir Patrick Spens' to 'Tamlane' to the tragic tale of 'Binoorie':

> She clasped her hands about a broom root,
> *Binoorie, O Binoorie;*
> But her cruel sister she loosed them out,
> By the bonnie mill-dams of Binoorie.

One librarian, Grace Hallworth, has tried chanting the ballad to chords on an auto-harp, thus reviving the way in which ballads were represented originally. Some teachers and librarians use a guitar to accompany more modern ballads to great effect.

'Tall tales', that is, stories in which the bounds of probability are stretched so far that the story becomes extravagant and amusing nonsense, are seldom used with children, although their humour is often a success with ten-to-eleven-year-olds. The classic examples are the tales by R. E. Raspe of the exploits of Baron Munchausen, published in 1785. Here we read of a hunter whose dog literally ran off its legs in the service of its master and so became a dachshund, and the hunter who shot a stag out of whose head a cherry tree was growing laden with fruit, so he had cherry pie for supper.

The modern examples of the 'Tall tale' come from America and are stories of fabulous heroes. Paul Bunyan's tales are typical: his ox measured 'forty-two axe-handles and a plug of chewing tobacco from tip to tip of its horns', and his hunters were so tall that they had to stand on ladders to shave themselves. Such tales are perhaps a natural product of the exuberance of the early frontiersmen and hunters in their new land. Examples can be found in Virginia Haviland's *North American Legends*.

Although fairy tales and fantasy of various kinds are the major source of stories for telling, some children prefer more realistic tales. For one child a broom is a witch's steed, for another merely something useful and everyday. The storyteller's repertoire must always include stories for the child who poses that awkward question, 'But is it true? Did it really happen?' Such children identify with boys and girls, heroes and heroines, who *do* something, who meet danger and achieve goals which are possible in what is called the 'real world'. Younger children enjoy Astrid Lindgren's stories of a natural and homely family in *The Bullerby Children*, or an episode from Eve Garnett's *The Family from One End Street* (old-fashioned, perhaps, but still enjoyable). The older group usually enjoy the story of a boy marooned by a snowstorm with Zlateh the goat, by Isaac Bashevis Singer, or a shortened version of *The Boy Who Was Afraid* by Armstrong Sperry, the story of a South Seas boy who was afraid of the sea. John Masefield's *Jim Davis*, an exciting smuggling story, can be told as a serial, while E. Nesbit's stories are rich in amusing episodes which can be told singly. For eleven-to-twelve-year-olds there are short stories like Bill Naughton's collection *The Goalkeeper's Revenge*, in which there is a tragic story of a boy, Spit Nolan—champion trolley-rider, who loses both the race and his life. From the realistic but fictitious story it is a natural step to true stories of exploration, natural disasters and of real people—Scott, Madame Curie, Mozart, Amy Johnson, Hans Andersen—anyone whose life makes a good story and about whom you, as storyteller, can feel enthusiasm.

Humorous stories should not be forgotten, for all children like to laugh. Such stories are welcome after the main story, providing an opportunity to relax. With the younger children try Joan Aiken's *Tales of Arabel's Raven*, a bird which has the awkward habit of shouting 'Nevermore' down telephones, or Rose Fyleman's 'The Magic Umbrella'. With the older boys and girls try a story from J. B. Haldane's *My Friend Mr Leakey* (a magician), Norman Hunter's 'Professor Branestawm' stories, or an episode from the amusing *The Phoenix and the Carpet* by E. Nesbit. Nonsense poems add spice—Edward Lear's verses, Belloc's *Cautionary Tales*,

31

Spike Milligan's *Silly Verse for Kids*. Consult Lance Salway's book list, *Humorous Books for Children*, for further suggestions.

Lastly there are what I call 'Granny stories', reminiscences told by an older person about his or her life and experiences. These can have a real value in bridging the gap between the generations and giving a child a sense of the continuity of time, always a difficult concept for young children. One father beginning a story with 'When I was a little boy. . .' was somewhat disconcerted when his young son said sagely, 'Oh, yes, when there were dinosaurs. . .'

There is such a wide variety of material from which to choose suitable stories! No wonder the storyteller sometimes makes mistakes—I remember with a shudder one of my own. Faced with twenty 'downtown' children aged five or so, I chose to show them the picture book *The Three Robbers* by Tomi Ungerer. Immediately a small boy in the front row jumped up and shouted 'Bang, bang!' and continued this refrain throughout my story—nothing would silence him and he was soon joined by a chorus of friends. But mistakes are the storyteller's fault and should always be regarded as warnings for the next time.

The final question we should always ask of ourselves in selection is 'What is it in this story that I want to share with children? Is it fun, beauty, excitement, interest in character, an underlying principle worthy of emulation?' Unless a story has some quality worth sharing, it is not worth telling.

It is impossible to say what makes one particular story yours, but I have found that suddenly a story leaps from the page and is alive and full of meaning for me. I know that it is *my* story and that I shall be able to tell it with conviction. This must have been the experience of every storyteller. By reading and telling, trial and error, I believe that gradually the storyteller develops a 'sixth sense'. In time you will *know* that a story is right for you as soon as you see it. When a story is yours in this way, it is reasonable to believe that it will please the children too, because you believe in it and can tell it with enthusiasm.

5

Adapting the Story for Telling

'Bold design, constant practice, frequent mistakes.'

John Masefield

Quite often when you have selected a suitable story, it is obvious that it will be difficult to tell as it stands. A story for telling needs a different construction and emphasis than a story written for reading to yourself. Added to this, most stories need to be modified to suit a particular audience or age-group. Experience shows that some adaptation is both legitimate and desirable.

The most common requirement is the shortening of a lengthy story to meet the limitations of time or the powers of concentration of a particular age-group. To try to condense too much into the time available gives a feeling of haste—storytelling should always be unhurried and relaxed—and may mean that the climax cannot be given its due impact. Usually a reasonable shortening is quite possible without spoiling the story as a whole; indeed most stories benefit from a little pruning.

One of the most obvious ways of doing this is to remove secondary ramifications of the plot, which should also help to keep the storyline clear. A good example is 'Volkh's Journey to the East' by E. M. Almedingen. The main plot concerns Volkh's wishes and the way they help him to win a seat among the Knights of the Golden Table, but at the very beginning of the story there is a secondary plot about

Volkh's mother and her most treasured possession. This has no significance for the main plot and can be omitted without spoiling the story. Another example is the Polish folk tale, 'The Jolly Tailor who Became King'. It contains a strange piece of folklore about the little tailor's visit to the devils' house, which can mean little to children. This can be omitted, for the story is complete, and indeed more suitable for children, without it. A brief analysis of the plot of any story will soon make it obvious when such asides can safely be discarded.

Unnecessarily detailed descriptive passages not only slow down the action, they also leave little scope for the child's imagination to come into play. One of the benefits of storytelling is that it provides a stimulus to the imagination; this is lost if every scene and person is described, as it would be in a film or on television. An adult's description of a princess, for instance, will probably fall far short of the child's own glamorous picture. A scene needs only a general description for the child to identify it with some place known to him and so visualise it to his own satisfaction. When reading alone, you can skip or read long descriptive passages as you wish but they cannot be ignored in a story that is told and may only serve to bore or confuse a child listener. Take this from the beginning of Walter de la Mare's story, 'The Three Sleeping Boys of Warwickshire':

> In a low-ceiled, white-washed room on the uppermost floor of a red-brick building in Pleasant Street, Cheriton, standing there in their glazed cases, is a collection of shells, conches, sea-weeds, dried salty sea flowers, fossils, staring birds, goggling fish with starry eyes . . .'

The child might well be forgiven for asking 'When are you going to begin the story?'

Sometimes a rearrangement of the sequence of events may be justified for the sake of clarity, or even an added event which has been implied but not told. In the original version of Rose Fyleman's 'The Magic Umbrella', the old woman's sudden flight to the top of the church steeple is only stated as a possibility. So many children asked 'But why hasn't she gone to the top of the steeple?' that I was forced to add this crowning absurdity in my own words; this has become an essential part of the story in all subsequent retellings.

Whatever else is deleted, repetitive phrases must be retained because of the attraction they have for children and the invitation to participate which they offer. How much tamer the story of 'The Gingerbread Man' would be if it did not have the refrain, 'Run, run, as fast as you can, You can't catch me, I'm the Gingerbread Man'—children can never resist joining in with gusto. Would the story of 'The Three Pigs' have had the same appeal if the sinister Wolf had never growled, 'Then I'll huff and I'll puff and I'll blow your house down'? There is no doubt that the popularity of the story of Henny-Penny is largely due to the repetition of the names of her companions: Cocky-locky, Ducky-daddles, Goosey-poosey, Turkey-lurkey and the villainous Foxy-woxy.

The opening is particularly important when telling a story. Most stories, particularly folk tales, begin with some variant of 'Once upon a time', a phrase which establishes the non-time of the story, a magic far-away time in which anything can happen. The first few sentences should always give some indication of what the story is going to be about:

> There was once a poor widow who had an only son named Jack, and a cow named Milky-white, and she was their only fortune . . .

This kind of down-to-earth opening is found in most folk tales. It is even better, however, if the first sentence excites the child's expectations of what is to come. Take this from Andersen's 'The Tinder Box':

> A soldier came marching along the high road, left, right, left, right. He had his knapsack on his back and a sword at his side, for he had been to the wars and was returning home. And on the road he met a Witch—a horrid-looking creature . . .

35

Or this intriguing opening from a Russian fairy tale, 'To Your Good Health':

Long, long ago there lived a king who was such a mighty monarch that whenever he sneezed everyone in the whole country had to say 'To your good health!' Everyone said it except the shepherd with the bright blue eyes, and he would *not* say it . . .

First sentences as they stand are not always a good introduction, for the author may not have had the experience in mind of telling a story to a group of restless children! It may be necessary, therefore, to write your own first sentence. If so, make it as arresting as you can and commit it to memory so firmly that it makes a confident opening that bridges the apprehensive moment before the story has got underway.

Equally important for success is the final sentence of a story, for this is largely responsible for the impression which remains in the child's mind. It must fit the story, leaving no ragged ends. Whether it is tragic or comic, the listening child should feel satisfied that all is well, the quest over, the evil thing conquered, the 'good' characters living happily:

Out of the bag jumped little Dog Turpie and he ate up all the Hobyahs. And that is why there are no Hobyahs left anywhere in the world.

Such reassurance is very important for little children.

The Hungarian tale of 'The Witch and the Swan Maiden' has a similarly reassuring ending which is likely to appeal to older children:

The witch filled the room with darkness: the people sat and shuddered in the darkness; the king and queen clung together; and when the darkness lifted, the witch had vanished.

So the king, the queen and the little prince lived in great happiness ever after.

But an ending such as this from Andersen's 'The Little Mermaid' is too vague and descriptive to be really satisfactory:

We fly invisibly through the dwellings of men, where there are no children: and wherever we find a good child, who gives pleasure to his parents and deserves their love, the good God shortens their time of probation . . .

You should always try to convey a feeling of finality at the end of a story and this can often be achieved by intonation alone. At other times a slight rephrasing or transposing of words is effective. As an example, consider this from Patrick Chalmer's 'The Little Pagan Faun':

Now you mayn't be able to believe that the Lady promised the little pagan faun anything of the sort, but *I* can assure you that she did, and that he trotted off into the woods again, munching his cake and feeling much comforted about things, just as the clocks were striking twelve and it was Christmas Day.

This is too wordy and does not have the impact and finality the story needs. What is important to remember is that the little pagan faun is comforted and that it is Christmas Day. So try this:

So the little pagan faun trotted off into the woods again, munching his cake and feeling much comforted. At that very moment the clocks struck twelve. It was CHRISTMAS DAY!

Endings should always be brief and to the point, for once the climax has been reached, the child inevitably tends to lose interest.

Some details in traditional material may seem too gruesome for children and if so, they should be omitted or toned down. The gory fights between Beowulf and the monster Grendel in the Anglo-Saxon epic poem, or the 'battle frenzies' in the Irish hero stories, are very often disturbing, and many folk tales are strewn with blood-curdling episodes. One of the most gruesome is 'Mr Fox': when Lady Mary goes into Mr Fox, her fiancé's, house, she sees: 'bodies and skeletons of beautiful young ladies all stained with blood . . . The sword cut off the hand, which jumped up into the air, and fell into Lady Mary's lap.' More subtle but peculiarly chilling is Andersen's 'The Red Shoes', in which a vain girl who goes to her confirmation wearing red shoes is condemned to dance the world over until 'she is pale and cold and her skin shrinks and crumples up like a skeleton's'. Although the executioner cuts off her feet, the red shoes dance on.

Some children may gloat over such details, but this is generally mere bravado. With an audience of young children in mind, it may be as well to avoid such endings as the version of 'Cinderella' where the ugly sisters' eyes are plucked out by pigeons, or Perrault's retelling of 'The Sleeping Beauty' in which the princess' mother-in-law plans to eat her own grandchildren.

However, you should always be aware of being too guarded—children often seem to accept punishments at the end of traditional folk tales as being well deserved and do not visualise them in all their horror as an adult might. Certainly, stories which feature dragons or other monsters having their heads cut off do not usually upset children, as long as such punishments are mentioned matter-of-factly and not enlarged upon. They are on a par with the Red Queen of Hearts' 'Off with their heads!'

Can we—and ought we—to introduce a book we should like children to read by telling a part of it freely? I dislike 'retold' classics which reduce a book notable for its style to a rehash of what is possibly not a very good plot. Dickens and the Brontës, who are the most common victims of this process, did not write for children, and their books are probably best saved until the child can read them for himself. But when the book in question *was* intended for children yet presents

38

difficulties to the average child-reader, there may be a case for adapting it to make it more accessible. A prime example is *The Water Babies*; the story of the little chimney sweep who becomes a water baby has great appeal for children, but the style is overloaded with period verbiage and moral reflections which can be offputting. Try retelling the first part; your audience will very likely be inspired to venture on the rest of the book on their own. Similarly E. Nesbit's books are well worth introducing for their comedy and characters, in spite of their rather unattractive appearance to a modern child. An episode from *The Phoenix and the Carpet*, for instance, never fails. Only certain books lend themselves to retelling in this way; if in doubt, read selected passages from the book itself.

An interesting problem is what to do with stories told in the first person. Eleanor Farjeon's story of 'Bertha Goldfoot' is told by an old nurse; Masefield's smuggling story, *Jim Davis*, by a boy of fourteen or so; J. B. S. Haldane's 'A Meal with a Magician' by an unknown young man. The storyteller is unlikely to resemble any of these people, so is it incongruous to tell these stories from the point of view of their protagonists? Is it possible that to imply that the story is happening to oneself may get in the way of the child's own identification with the hero or heroine? It is well known that most children don't like what they call 'I' books. It may seem wiser to tell such stories in reported speech, but this decision must be made afresh for each story of this kind. 'A Meal with a Magician', for instance, undoubtedly gains impact and authenticity by being told as a personal experience, especially as the narrator is largely anonymous and all attention is focused on the remarkable happenings. After telling this amusing story in the first person, I have had children ask me, as Mr Leakey's friend, to tell them where he lived so that they could go there and perhaps catch a glimpse of Pompey the dragon or Oliver the octopus.

To sum up: for telling, a story must have a pattern which comprises an inviting beginning, not too many characters,

39

a logical sequence of events—that is, not a series of arbitrary events which have little connection with each other—plenty of action and a satisfying ending. The story should build up to a climax quickly followed by the ending. One of the most lively storytellers, John Masefield, said 'Remarkable openings, proper pauses, notable climaxes, make a good story.'

An example of such a pattern is Andersen's 'The Real Princess'. Brief as it is, there is an intriguing beginning with a prince searching for a real princess; the arrival of a girl in a dramatic storm who, in spite of appearances, claims that she is a real princess; the ingenious test the queen sets for her and the triumphant climax when the princess proves her royal status by feeling a pea through a mountain of mattresses and eiderdowns. The classic happy ending is followed by the sentence which establishes the authenticity of the story—the actual pea can be seen in the royal museum.

Even after subsequent retellings when you have established the pattern of the story and its details, you will find that further changes have crept into the story, almost without your knowledge, because of the reaction of the audience. An extra minor character has been introduced, another character has disappeared, details have been added or omitted, frightening incidents have been toned down for the sake of some sensitive child. Whatever additions and subtractions have been made, the basic story remains the same and keeps its identity. It has merely been shaped by the storyteller and the response of the audience. That is as it should be and as it always has been.

6

Remembering the Story

'His story finished, through and through,
Its scenes still sweet in memory, too,
He'd shut his book, a moment sit,
Inwardly musing over it . . .'
Walter de la Mare (*Books*)

It is seldom necessary to learn a story word for word, and this
is particularly true of folk tales. There is no definitive version
of these old tales, for until the last century they were handed
down by word of mouth. No doubt storytellers in every
generation make slight alterations, while always retaining
the basic pattern. New versions appear constantly, so the
storyteller is free to tell the tales in his own words.

A story learnt by rote is not usually as absorbing for
the audience as one told in the storyteller's own words so
that it seems spontaneous. Memorising can cause self-
consciousness and a memorised story can often sound like a
recitation. It is also risky, for any sudden interruption can
break the storyteller's concentration and cause a loss of
memory. This is disconcerting, not only for the storyteller
but also for the children who find it difficult to pick up the
thread of the story again.

Although the keynote of storytelling is spontaneity, this
does not mean that the storyteller is improvising—far from
it. What it does mean is that the story has become so much a
part of yourself that it flows freely. Imagine the basic work of
preparation as the trunk of a tree, firmly based and very
much alive. As the story is absorbed, the tree branches freely
and breaks naturally into leaves of imagination—but these
are still part of the tree itself.

How to set about remembering a story? There are many methods, according to the kind of memory each individual has. Generally speaking, however, it would seem that there is a basic pattern to follow. First read the story to yourself two or three times, once for the story only, the second time concentrating on its *construction*. Notice how it works up to its climax, how it *feels* as to mood, how it ends. Now is the time to jot down an outline of the story and the names of the characters as you remember them. The very act of writing these down helps to fix them in the memory. Comparing the outline with the original, it may surprise you to discover what you have missed.

Studying the story in more detail, make a note of repetitive phrases which are vital to the story and must be retained. Wanda Gag knew the value of repetition for encouraging children to participate. Her 'Hundreds of cats, thousands of cats, millions and billions and trillions of cats', must have been chanted by untold numbers of children. Or take a cumulative story like 'The Turnip' which in Elizabeth Clark's version runs like this:

And the little Mouse had hold of the little black and white Cat, the little black and white Cat had hold of the little Girl the grandchild, and the little Girl the grandchild had hold of the little old Woman the grandmother, and the little old Woman the grandmother had hold of the little old Man her husband, and the little old Man her husband had hold of the Turnip; and they pulled, and they pulled, and they pulled, and *up* came the Turnip!

There may also be phrases which help to show character, and these are worth noting down. In 'Tom Tit Tot', for example, the simple daughter says to herself of the pies, ' "Well, if they'll come again, I'll eat 'em now." And she set to work and ate 'em all, first and last.'

As the story begins to take shape in your mind, it is helpful to visualise it so that you can see it as a series of colourful, moving pictures. If the storyteller cannot see the story, neither will the audience. It does not necessarily follow that the children see the same mental picture as the storyteller, but this does not seem to matter. This was brought home to me when I was telling stories to blind children who could not possibly visualise what I was seeing, yet were obviously content with their imaginings. You have only to think of such an everyday sight as a river, to realise how differently it can appear to each of us. In a story each child sees a river he knows and which seems right to him. If it were possible to look into each child's imagination when telling a story you would see an astonishing variety of images.

As an experiment try to visualise a story you know well: Andersen's 'The Nightingale', for instance. Stand with the courtiers and the kitchen maid as they wait in the forest to hear the Nightingale sing. Imagine the scene in the palace as the emperor waits condescendingly for the Nightingale to appear. Look at the artificial Nightingale and listen to its song. What do you see? What do you hear? Building up a mental picture full of sound and colour is a great help in remembering a story.

As we become familiar with a story, the characters develop into real people. Because we know them, their adventures are easier to remember. In 'Epaminondas', the familiar story of the child who 'hasn't got the sense he was born with', so always applies his aunt's sensible suggestions too late, with ludicrous results, each incident is linked to the next so the story is easily memorised. With more compli- cated stories, the plot can usually be divided into sections so that the logical progress of events is clear and more easily memorised. This approach may seem too clinical, but it is only a temporary device to aid the memory.

Now you are ready to tell the story *aloud* to yourself or to anyone who will listen. This is the only way to discover the places in the story where the right words don't come 'trip- pingly on the tongue' and where your memory is failing you. Only when you no longer need to think about the words you are to use can you be sure that you really know the story.

Words are to the storyteller what notes of music are to the composer or paint to the artist. Listen to this from Malory's *Morte D'Arthur:*

> 'Therefore,' said Arthur unto Sir Bedivere, 'take thou Excalibur my good sword, and go with it to yonder water side, and when thou comest there I charge thee throw my sword in that water, and come again and tell me what thou seest . . .'

Here the choice of words gives a strong sense of period, and even if 'thee' and 'thou' are replaced by 'you' this passage still retains its authentic ring.

Or this, from Wanda Gag's *Gone is Gone.* Here is a different world, the countryside in a folk tale:

> The sky was blue, the sun right gay and golden, and the flowers they were like angels' eyes blinking in the grass . . .

The way in which words are used plays an important part in establishing the mood of the story. The following passage from Oscar Wilde's 'The Selfish Giant' shows the sudden change from the happy atmosphere of the garden to the threatening return of the Giant:

> It was a large and lovely garden, with soft green grass. Here and there over the grass grew beautiful flowers like stars, and there were twelve peach-trees that in the spring-time broke into delicate blossoms of pink and pearl, and in the autumn bore rich fruit. The birds sat on the trees and sang so sweetly that the children used to stop their games in order to listen to them. 'How happy we are!' they cried to each other.
>
> One day the Giant came back . . .

Should we use slang when telling fairy tales? Is it fitting that a Prince should say 'O.K.' or that Boots should get 'real mad'? To me, this is pantomime language and quite out of place in the magic atmosphere of a fairy tale. Although archaic language is obviously unsuitable for modern children, the storyteller should always be sensitive to the feeling of a story and the words she uses to tell it.

While there is a rich variety of stories which can be told in one's own words, there are some stories which must retain the author's words in their entirety. Kipling's *Just So Stories* are an obvious example. Could any other words be used for 'The Elephant's Child'?

> Before he thought what he was doing, he schlooped up a schloop of mud from the banks of the grey-green, greasy Limpopo river and slapped it on his head, where it made a cool, schloopy-slushy mudcap all tickly behind the ears.

Similarly, beautifully written stories by masters of their craft should never be reproduced in the storyteller's own, relatively inadequate language. Walter de la Mare, Laurence Housman, Rumer Godden and Eleanor Farjeon are examples in this connection. On the whole, Walter de la Mare's stories are more suitable for reading than telling because of their contemplative style, but his imaginative re-tellings of familiar fairy tales in the collection entitled *Tales Told Again*, are well worth telling—in the author's words. They are more direct and shorter than the bulk of his work, and their content is familiar. Laurence Housman's collections of short stories include a few that are very popular with children, particularly 'A Chinese Fairy Tale' in which an artist steps into his own picture and walks along its painted paths to disappear for three hundred years.

Of Rumer Godden's tales I would recommend *The Mousewife*, a perfect and charming story inspired by a passage in Dorothy Wordsworth's diary. The mousewife is different from the other mice, and she is dissatisfied with her lot, although she doesn't quite know why. A captive dove tells her of the woods and fields and how it feels to fly, for she is a house mouse and knows nothing of the world outside. In her compassion for her friend, the mousewife sets the dove free:

> He did not see her or look towards her, then—clap—he took her breath away so that she fell. He had opened his wings and flown straight out. For a moment he dipped as if he would fall, his wings were cramped, and then he moved them and lifted up and up and flew away across the tops of the trees.
> The mousewife picked herself up and shook out her bones and fur. 'So that is to fly,' she said. 'Now there is no one to tell me about the hills and the corn and the clouds . . .'

For me this story has all the compassion, integrity and skilful economy of words so characteristic of Rumer Godden.

Eleanor Farjeon's 'Elsie Piddock Skips in her Sleep' was written in her Sussex cottage as children skipped in the lane outside. It was her favourite story amongst the many she wrote, for she felt that it said more 'what she wanted to say' than any others. It is the story of Elsie Piddock who, when she was a child, skipped with the fairies and who, when she was 109 years old, saved Mount Caburn for the children of Glynde and for the fairies by her magical skipping. She is still skipping and:

> . . . If you go to Caburn at the new moon, you may catch a glimpse of a tiny bent figure, no bigger than a child, skipping all by itself in its sleep, and hear a gay little voice, like the voice of a dancing yellow leaf, singing: 'ANdy SPANdy SUGARdy CANdy, FRENCH ALmond ROCK!'

I cannot tell this story without remembering the lively, affectionate person who was Eleanor Farjeon.

Telling stories like these is more difficult than telling a folk tale, but it is infinitely worthwhile for both storyteller and audience. It demands not only experience but empathy with

46

the author. I have had the good fortune to have known both
Rumer Godden and Eleanor Farjeon as friends for many
years, but it is not necessary, of course, to know an author
personally in order to capture the essence of a story. To alter
the way in which stories of this calibre are written would be
impertinence. A little abridging *may* be legitimate but that is all.

The best stories deserve telling more than once. We may
want to repeat them many times, sometimes with long intervals between each telling. One of the best ways to remind
yourself of them quickly is to keep a story notebook in which
you enter the outlines of those stories which have proved
worthy of telling again. It can be as detailed as you have time
for—the more detailed it is the easier it will be to recover the
story from your memory. It is also useful to compile a subject
index so that you can find suitable stories for a particular
occasion.

Here is an example of an entry in one of my story
notebooks:

The Three Sillies

Source: *English Fairy Tales* Joseph Jacobs (Bodley Head)

PART ONE

Opening Sentence

'Once upon a time there was a farmer and his wife and they
had one daughter, and she was courted by a gentleman.'

Gentleman visits farm each evening, girl goes down to
cellar to draw beer for him. One evening she notices an axe
sticking in the beam over her head.

Quote 'Supposing him and me was to be married and we was
to have a son and he was to come down into the cellar to
draw beer like as I'm doing now, and that there axe was to
fall on his head and kill him, what a dreadful thing it
would be!'

47

Sits down to cry.
a) Mother comes down—beer running over the floor. Asks daughter what is the matter. *Repeat Quote* Mother sits down to cry.
b) Father comes down—beer running all over the floor. Asks mother what is the matter. *Repeat Quote* Father sits down to cry.
c) Gentleman comes down. Sees beer all over the floor. Turns off tap of barrel. Asks father what is the matter. *Repeat Quote* Gentleman laughs, pulls out axe from beam, says: 'I've never met three such big sillies as you are. When I can find three bigger sillies than you three, I'll come back and marry your daughter.'

PART TWO

Gentleman sets out on travels. Comes to
a) Cottage where woman is trying to persuade cow to climb ladder to roof (where grass is growing). Tells her to climb ladder herself and throw grass down. She drives cow up ladder, ties rope round it, drops end down chimney and ties it round her waist. Cow falls, woman jerked up chimney. ONE BIG SILLY.
b) Man at inn gets up early each morning, fastens trousers to knobs on chest-of-drawers, runs and tries to jump into them. Gentleman suggests proper way to put on trousers. TWO BIG SILLIES.
c) Villagers trying to rescue moon from pond with rakes, brooms, pitchforks. Gentleman tells them it is only *reflection* of moon in pond. Villagers chase him away. THREE BIG SILLIES.

Concluding Sentence

'So the gentleman turned back home again and married the farmer's daughter, and if they didn't live happily ever after, that's nothing to do with you or me.'

So the process of memorising a story means very much more than just reading it through a short while before you are to tell it. In order to tell it effectively the storyteller must see it in her imagination, hear what the characters are saying, feel what they are feeling—and be prepared to spend time and energy on learning it. Practice and experience enable the storyteller to bring out the full potential of a story. Once it is absorbed in this way it becomes a personal experience and a new creation every time you tell it. The very fact that it has not been learnt word for word, but has become part of you, means that there is no necessity to use the same words every time—the storyteller is free and so is the story.

7

Improving Your Voice and Speech

'Speak the speech, I pray you, as I pronounced
it to you, trippingly on the tongue . . .'

Hamlet

After the adaptation of the story itself, there comes the actual
telling and here *voice*, that is, the way in which you produce
your voice, and *diction*, the degree of clarity with which you
speak, are all important. As with making a speech, it is not
only what is said but *how* it is said that makes storytelling a
success or failure. Some knowledge and skill on 'how to get it
over' is essential. The storyteller needs to know how to use
her voice, for this is the instrument on which much of the
story's impact depends. It is the storyteller's responsibility
to make sure her voice is audible. If children have to strain to
hear what you are saying, they will soon lose interest.

A pleasantly modulated voice is a gift, but much can be
done to improve any voice, especially when there are particular difficulties. Most voices need strengthening. Even
when speaking to small groups it is not enough to use a
conversational tone, it must be 'enlarged'. Actors can, by
using their voices in the right way, be heard distinctly in
every part of the theatre and the storyteller must learn this
skill.

The quickest way to learn how to use the voice correctly, of
course, is to have a few lessons in voice production. Informa-
tion about private teachers of speech can be found in the
local press, or there may be an evening class at a local centre.

Particulars of such classes are always available in libraries. For myself I found that three terms with a private teacher who concentrated on teaching me how to use my voice and how to breathe correctly—and who enjoyed listening to stories and did not try to teach me an 'elocutionary' style—was an excellent investment. As a result I have never suffered from a strained throat—but if such lessons are impossible here are a few hints that may be helpful.

Easy and correct breathing, properly controlled, is the foundation of good speaking. Most people breathe shallowly from the top of the chest. This results in tightness and any attempt to increase volume causes strain. Practise breathing from the diaphragm, feeling the expansion of the lower ribs with your hands as you breathe and filling the lungs to capacity. This will help to develop a good clear tone. Humming is a useful exercise, using the vowel sounds, first with the letter 'M' before them and then with 'B'. This helps to improve nasal resonance and it is this which produces a musical quality in the voice.

Every member of your audience must be able to hear you; however, this does not mean that you need to shout or use a 'booming' voice. Indeed, this often distorts and confuses the sound of words. Beware of 'talking to yourself' or telling the story to the front row only. Direct your voice to the back of the room and lift your head so that you can see everyone there. Think of your breath as coming from directly in front of your face, rather than from your throat and you will find that gradually you will be able to 'throw' your voice so that it carries to the back of the room. This is not forcing the voice—to do so would result in a strained throat—but is a gentle and gradual process helped by thinking carefully about what you are trying to do.

A knowledge of how to control your breathing so that you make the best possible use of your voice, helps to give confidence in telling a story. If you are concerned that the audience cannot hear you or worried that your voice may fail, this will very likely lead to a feeling of tension which will not only affect you, but the story and the audience as well. Clear speaking and pronunciation are essential so that storytelling becomes a pleasure for everyone concerned.

Clear diction is also essential. Slurred or clipped words, slipshod speech, make it difficult for those listening. As an exercise, try saying nursery rhymes aloud, slowly at first and then at varying speeds. Tongue-twisters, jingles and nonsense verses like Lewis Carroll's 'Lobster Quadrille' or 'Jabberwocky' will all help in the mastery of clear speech, for they must be carefully spoken. Be wary, however, not to develop the habit of exaggerated 'mouthing' of the words as some singers do. Overdone pronunciation is unpleasant to watch and to hear. You should aim to develop a natural way of speech that is both clear and pleasant.

A common fault is dropping the voice at the end of a sentence. This 'falling inflection' makes for a sing-song delivery—a sure way to send the audience to sleep. It may also mean that children miss a vital word which is necessary for the understanding of the story. For example: 'Once upon a time there was a man and his wife who had but one son and he was blind . . .' Drop your voice on that vital word 'blind' so that it is not heard and many children will lose the key to the story.

Have you ever listened to your voice on a tape-recorder? It will be a salutary experience, revealing unrealised faults and a wrong use of the voice. Note whether you have a tendency to speak monotonously or in a minor key—this can sound depressing—to stumble over words or to fill a pause with 'er'. All these drawbacks can be overcome once you are conscious of them.

Everyone must have suffered from the public speaker who delivers his whole speech at the same level of voice and pace. Very soon the message, however well prepared and significant, ceases to have any meaning for those listening. Constant variety in pace and pitch is vital if your audience is to remain alert and responsive.

Obviously, pace and tone depend upon the kind of story

you are telling. Compare a story such as Andersen's gently satirical 'The Nightingale' with the vigorous, down-to-earth folk tale 'Molly Whuppie' and it will be obvious that the two differ as much in pace as they do in mood. It is as well to start any story fairly slowly to give the audience time to become used to your voice and personality. To hurry unduly through nervousness means that some children are unable to follow the story; to tell a story too slowly is tedious and uninteresting for the listener. A judicious blend of variety in pace and tone makes a story more interesting and easier to listen to. The human voice has infinite potential for expressing mood and character. Youth and age, timidity and courage, king and peasant, can all be suggested by the tone and pitch of the voice, as well as by small mannerisms and choice of words.

In spite of all your preparation, you will almost certainly feel a little nervous before telling a story. This happens to the most experienced storytellers, and oddly enough, is an advantage, for a little nervousness tends to heighten your sensibility and awareness. It helps to take a deep breath. Look round your audience in a friendly way—it isn't their fault if you are feeling inadequate and fearful! The important thing is to make this first attempt—the second is never as difficult!

8

Facing the Audience

'Begin at the beginning . . . and go on till you
come to the end; then stop.'
          Lewis Carroll (*Alice in Wonderland*)

Whatever the occasion or venue, the practical question of
accommodation must always be the storyteller's first consid-
eration when preparing for a storytelling session. There are
two physical essentials for storytelling—a quiet place, free
from interruption, and comfortable conditions for both teller
and audience. Seldom is the storyteller blessed in this way
and she must always be ready to adjust to circumstances,
however unfavourable. Sometimes the only suitable place to
tell a story is in the corner of a busy room with at most a
screen of some kind to give the illusion of privacy. In an
open-plan school or library, a quiet spot may be hard to find,
and in a playgroup environment, where there may be only
one large room for all activities, it can be even harder. On
one occasion during a Book Week, I was allotted a 'quiet
corner' through which waves of noisy children, engaged in
more vigorous activities, swept in and out yelling so fiercely
that the younger children in my audience clustered round
me for reassurance. Another problem can be caused by
curious adults who, having disturbed the concentration of
the children, drift away again. Polite firmness is the only
answer to such interruptions.

As for comfortable conditions for the audience, it is
unreasonable to expect children to sit on the floor for any
length of time without fidgeting. Fidgeting is infectious and
causes unrest which disturbs both audience and storyteller.
If children must sit in a cramped position, make an interval

between stories for them to stretch their arms at least—or if it is possible, to stand up and turn round three times. Cushions are a help but are apt to be appropriated by the strongest, or used as weapons. Gaily coloured stools are much enjoyed by little children and are guarded jealously—they may be used as trains if unsupervised. Some modern libraries have tiered steps where children can sit quite comfortably. Avoid the formality of rows, for serried ranks of children can give a feeling of faceless anonymity. A semi-circle of seats is always preferable to straight rows, as long as it does not cover too wide an area. A gangway down the *centre* of the room makes it difficult for the storyteller to 'gather the eyes' of the audience. To be compelled to turn one's head from side to side like a demented weathercock in order to see the children is tiring for the storyteller and unrestful for everyone.

It would be reassuring to believe that an audience can always be restricted to a small number, ideally about twenty, but this is rarely the case. The storyteller must be prepared to tackle any number, according to circumstances. As a visiting storyteller to schools, my audience can vary from fifty to as many as three hundred, which is certainly not a desirable number. If at all possible, fifty is the maximum for intimate storytelling. Any greater number needs a storyteller of considerable experience and confidence, or it may get out of hand and become too impersonal.

Some storytellers like to sit in a comfortable chair when telling a story to suggest informality. Others stand—as I do myself—in order to see the audience more easily and to be free to move a little. Never sit or stand behind a table or lectern, for this creates a barrier between audience and storyteller. It is important to be able to see *all* the children and for them to see the storyteller. A faceless voice is much more difficult to listen to because of the lack of focus for the eyes and the attention. The storyteller should always try to sit or stand naturally, without fidgeting with anything, which may distract the children's attention from the

55

story. Storytelling should be restful to watch as well as to hear.

It may seem that these practical details are unimportant, but to neglect such matters is to risk disappointment when the story is told. An apparent informality is often a tribute to careful planning which allows a relaxed approach to the actual telling of the story.

And so the moment comes to face the audience. This is the test of all the selection and preparation that has gone before. The storyteller has no props, no costume, no scenery, only the story to share with the children. A live audience can be a terrifying experience and it is natural to feel nervous. However, if you remember that it is the story that matters, not yourself, it will help to banish self-consciousness.

First show the children the book the story comes from; it is important to establish firmly in children's minds the fact that books are a rich source of stories. It is prudent to introduce the story by some general phrase such as 'This is a story about finding treasure . . .' or 'This story is about a prince who had three wishes. . .' rather than by its title. If the title is familiar, some child will state uncompromisingly 'I've heard *that* story!' implying that he never wants to hear it again. This can be disconcerting to a storyteller who has painstakingly prepared a particular story and no other!

Preface the story by a brief explanation of anything that might puzzle children, for it is easy to assume that the audience is as knowledgeable as you are. While children should be stimulated to use their imagination and can easily *see* such fantastic creatures as fairies, giants or fabulous monsters, they cannot be expected to form a correct mental picture of a real animal they have never seen. So before telling a story such as Grey Owl's *The Adventures of Sajo and Her Beaver People*, it would be a good idea to show the children pictures of beavers and a lodge. Princes and princesses can be imagined much more romantically by children than by adults, but if the story is about a real person or place, some visual aid is needed.

No one can tell us exactly how to tell a story, for that is an individual matter which changes according to the individual personalities of different storytellers. Each person has a natural way of expressing what she wants to say and to copy someone else makes for insincerity. However, there are certain pitfalls and difficulties which the storyteller should be prepared for.

Avoid rhetorical questions with children of all ages, but particularly with young children. Very naturally children think that if someone asks a question, she wants an answer! 'He looked into the garden and what do you think he saw?' asks a storyteller in a playgroup. 'An elephant,' answers a boy confidently. 'No dear,' says the storyteller kindly, 'it was only a *small* garden.' 'It was a small elephant,' says the boy firmly. The story is ruined, for the kitten the storyteller meant to introduce is now an anti-climax. Every storyteller has had an experience like this.

And the interruptions! We are all familiar with the young child who says in the middle of a story, 'Look at my new shoes!' or 'Sometimes I wear yellow trowsis . . .' A story about a dog can elicit the comment, 'Our dog has a fur coat right down to his knees . . .' Theoretically such interruptions should be woven into the story, but this is not always humanly possible. There is one thing certain with an audience of young children, such comments cannot be ignored with impunity, for the child will persist until he receives some attention. What form this acknowledgement takes depends on the kind of interruption. It is usually completely irrelevant, in which case you can only say 'Yes, Mary!' or 'Tell me about it afterwards' or 'What fun!' and carry on with the story *immediately*. Usually the child is satisfied once he has been noticed. With older children, however, it is usually possible to establish a tradition that a story should not be interrupted because it breaks the continuity for the others. Occasionally this rule is broken catastrophi-

57

cally—on one occasion when I was telling the story of 'Lazy Tok' I said, quoting from the book, 'Shen mao tung shi—that's Chinese . . .' 'No it isn't!' came a voice from the audience, that of a Chinese boy from Hong Kong. I lost face, decidedly.

When showing a picture book to young children it is essential that all of them can see it easily; otherwise their cries of 'Can't see!' 'Show *me!*' can turn into quite violent protests. Always allow time for the picture to be absorbed and some comments to be made—'I don't like that picture, I can't tell what it is.' 'My Auntie wears a yellow jumper like that . . .'

Sometimes, participation is welcome and differs from interruption in that it implies absorption rather than inattention and involves the audience in the story. Little children love making train or animal noises, but take care that this doesn't get out of hand, especially if the animal in question is a pig! Older children enjoy an occasional chant or nonsense rhyme in which they can participate. 'Did you Feed my Cow?', 'I went to the Animal Fair', or 'What did you put in your Pocket?' (to be found in my hardback collections of stories), can all give shared pleasure.

Gesture can be a problem. How much should the storyteller use? If you are really 'in' the story, gesture and facial expression will come naturally, just as they do in conversation, and will arise spontaneously from the story itself. For example, length, height and direction call for a simple explanatory gesture. However, beware of exaggerated gestures, for they can easily look ludicrous. I shall never forget a visiting storyteller who recited Walter de la Mare's 'Off the Ground':

> Three jolly Farmers
> Once bet a pound
> Each dance the others would
> Off the ground . . .

She acted every movement suggested in the poem and

became so exhausted that I had to help her up from the platform. Her extravagant actions at first excited the children to laughter, then to obvious boredom. Storytelling, if made too dramatic, becomes a performance, for overdramatisation centres attention on the storyteller rather than the story.

Dialect—and by dialect I mean any kind of colloquial speech, unfamiliar idioms, odd or ungrammatical speech —is often a difficulty, for some stories can lose their impact if told without it. Consider the 'Brer Rabbit' stories. Imagine such a sentence as 'Brer Fox, he wink his eye slow, en lay low, en de Tar-Baby she ain't sayin' nuthin' ', translated into everyday grammatical speech. What it would lose! Such a tale as 'Tom Tit Tot' seems colourless in 'standard' English in comparison with the Suffolk dialect: 'That were grinning from ear to ear, an lawk! how that twirled that's tail!' If it seems impossible to imitate the intonation and distinctive vowel sounds of a dialect, it is better to leave such stories alone rather than use a 'phoney' accent. In many stories, however, it is sufficient to suggest the part of the country from which a story comes by a turn of phrase or a local word. 'Thee do movey, do'ee,' says the woodcutter in Somerset as he chops the dragon in half. 'Only mortal this dragon is, 'tis brave you are!' exclaims a lad in a Welsh tale. 'EE-ee!' says a man from Lancashire, 'You're nobbut a child!' 'Yon's a wee tyke!' remarks someone from Northumberland. But always remember that too much dialect can puzzle a child from another country—or even county.

As you begin telling the story you will realise that the time spent deciding upon the opening sentence was not wasted; the fact that you know it so well will help to overcome your nervousness. Suddenly the story gathers momentum and takes over from the storyteller. You should be there *in* the story, able to see the characters and take part in their adventures. As you near the climax of the story, there comes 'a catch of the breath, a beat and lifting of the heart' as Tolkien describes it. This is helped by the use of what actors call the dramatic pause, a slowing down and pause just before the climax. Your audience will hang breathlessly on such a pause, and even if some children have already guessed what is going to happen next, it will enable other, perhaps slower children to realise it too. A good example is found in 'Where Arthur Sleeps', in which a thief has to edge round a great bronze bell for, if he rings it, Arthur's knights will wake up. Inch by inch he edges round it . . . inch . . . by . . . inch. What will happen? A similar tension is found in 'Fierce Feathers', when into the silent Quaker Meeting House come fourteen Redskins in full war paint with poisoned arrows held taut to bow strings . . . !

After the climax of the story the ending should follow quickly. The response to the story can be unexpected! On one occasion when I had just told an exciting story, there was a moment of silence and then a boy leapt to his feet and cried, 'Three Cheers! Hip-hip-hip . . !' and the whole company of two hundred children joined in a deafening cheer. This was quite unpremeditated, a spontaneous release from the tension of an exciting story.

The greatest tribute that can be paid to a story is the moment of silence that sometimes follows. Such a moment of emotion and delight, the recognition of a perfect story, can come after stories of the calibre of Laurence Housman's 'A Chinese Fairy Tale' or Eleanor Farjeon's 'Elsie Piddock Skips in her Sleep'. The child has been lost in another world and it takes a little time to return to the everyday. Let him have that interlude. Don't spoil his pleasure and the impression left on heart and mind by at once intruding the mundane. To be told immediately and abruptly 'Time to go home! Put away your chairs and go out quietly', is to destroy something irrecoverable.

But after most stories there can be as many comments and questions as time allows. 'Are there any dinosaurs now?' asks one little girl. 'No silly, they have all gone to heaven!' replies another child piously. 'That was a heart-rending story!' says an older girl sniffing surreptitiously. 'Now I call

Long John Silver a *proper* pirate!' comments a boy, drawing his hand suggestively across his throat. 'Don't you worry about that dragon,' say two little boys wearing firemen's helmets and carrying rubber axes, 'We'll chop it up for you!' And after a story to introduce Erich Kästner's *Emil and the Detectives*, a boy says 'If Emil's mother had sent the money by postal order instead of giving it to Emil to take by train, there wouldn't have been all that trouble.' (Neither would there have been any story!) The storyteller should always be ready to listen to comments made by children, not only out of natural friendly interest, but because such observations are helpful in judging the impact of the story.

If the story has really become part of you, you will find that something else has happened—you are able to tell it while at the same time watching the reaction of the audience. Is the story too long? Does its humour really appeal to children? Perhaps a certain passage that seemed particularly good in preparation is not, in fact, so effective, for the children look puzzled. Has the fate of the wicked stepmother or the sudden appearance of a ghostly creature frightened some of the children?—if so, it must be toned down next time. Perhaps, on the other hand, the story has been made too tame for the children for the sake of satisfying adult sensibilities? You can learn a great deal about the story—and yourself—by watching critically how it is received.

A word of warning. A storyteller should realise that she has power which must never be used for its own sake. To tell stories of the trivial kind found in children's annuals or comics, which depend for their impact on sensationalism or crude humour; to make fun at the expense of authority; to present a story with exaggerated gestures in order to excite easy laughter, is to reduce storytelling to the lowest level of entertainment. This is 'playing to the gallery', which may well gain applause for the storyteller and provide a superficial and transitory pleasure for the audience, but it is a sad misuse of the power that 'Story' gives us and is not the purpose of storytelling. Sincerity and integrity are essential in any relationship with children. It is our privilege to be the medium through which children hear stories that give them lasting enjoyment, stories of adventure and danger, stories that amuse, stories which with their beauty and compassion are an emotional experience and touch the hearts of both storyteller and child.

In Haiti, when a storyteller feels he has a story to tell, he says to the audience 'Cric?' If he is approved, the people respond 'Crac!' and he can tell his story. If not, he must yield his place to another storyteller.

May your 'Cric?' always be answered by 'Crac!'

9

Special Situations

There are all kinds of activities centred on books each year, organised by libraries and schools, publishers, the National Book League and the Federation of Books for Your Children Groups. They appear under many names from 'Book Fairs' to 'Book Bangs', and storytelling takes place at most of them. The Federation also sponsors an annual 'Tell a Story Week', during which the emphasis is on storytelling in the many groups up and down the country.

Two specific occasions during the year which are observed in schools and libraries all over the world and by the Federation of Books for Your Children Groups in Britain, are Hallowe'en and Christmas, both of which offer excellent opportunities for storytelling.

Hallowe'en, traditionally the evening when ghosts and demons roam the land, is obviously an ideal time for stories about witches and ghosts. Such stories are doubly effective when told by the light of a candle in a turnip lantern. (Melons are easier to carve but when overheated, their smell is appalling!) It is also worth decorating the room with a background of witches, broomsticks and black cats to create a suitably festive atmosphere, and encouraging the children to dress up as witches and ghosts. Suitable stories can be found in Ruth Manning-Sanders' *A Book of Witches* and *A Book of Sorcerers and Spells* and in my own *Hallowe'en Acorn*. Eerie poems can add atmosphere—try e. e. cummings' 'hist whist', with its shattering closing 'WheeE E E!'. Barbara Ireson has compiled an anthology of witchy poems called *Shadows and Spells* which is very useful for such occasions.

Ghost stories are also very popular with children. The pleasure derived from these tales is compounded of a love of the mysterious and the unexplained—a ghost tale which is rationalised is not worth telling—and an element of fear of what may happen. Obviously stories of this kind must be told with caution, or indignant parents may descend upon the storyteller. However, as long as the atmosphere is festive and not too serious—as it should be at Hallowe'en—and there are adults around to give a feeling of security, ghost stories are innocuous. There are many collections available, from Ruth Manning-Sanders' *A Book of Ghosts and Goblins* to the much more subtle and chilling *The Shadow-Cage and Other Tales of the Supernatural* by Philippa Pearce.

Children half believe in these stories. I remember telling a ridiculous tale called *The Water Ghost* to a group of children. In it a ghost appeared annually, dripping water over the carpets of a stately home. It was finally 'laid' by the twentieth-century heir—he had it frozen and placed in cold storage. After the story was over several children asked me quite seriously for the telephone number of the cold storage firm so that they could ring up and enquire whether the water ghost was still immobilised!

For older children, Dickens' 'The Signalman' is notable for its eeriness and feeling of doom:

> I ran towards the figure, calling 'What's wrong? What has happened?' It stood just outside the entrance to the tunnel. I advanced so close to it that I wondered at its keeping the sleeve across its eyes. I ran right up to it and had my hand stretched out to pull the sleeve away—there was no one there.

A very unusual ghost story is Joan Aiken's 'Humble-puppy'. The narrator hears a sound and looks inside a deed box bought at an auction. Nothing there. The noise persists and as she puts her hand into the box again she feels 'a small, bony, warm, trembling body with big awkward feet, and silky dangling ears, and a cold nose . . .' It is a ghost puppy!

Or what about this for an encore, surely the most laconic ghost story in existence, a West Country folk tale:

> There were two fellows out working in a field, hoeing turnips they was, and the one he stop and lean on his hoe and he mop his face and he say, 'Yur—I don't believe in these yur ghostesses!'
> And t'other man say, 'Don't 'ee?'
> AND HE VANISHED.

Christmas is another universal children's festival when stories are welcome, set against the background of a Christmas tree. Many Christmas stories are to be found hidden away in collections of folk tales and it is worth keeping a note of any that appeal to you when you come across them. Ruth Sawyer's 'Schnitzle, Schnotzle and Schnootzle' is an enjoyable story and Elizabeth Clark has quite a number in her various collections, notably the story of 'Brother Johannick and his Silver Bell', a legend from Brittany in *Tales of Jack and Jane*. Children often enjoy hearing the same story again and again. In my own library it became a tradition to tell Ursula Moray Williams' *The Good Little Christmas Tree* every year. It is the story of a little tree which in its compassion for two children whose parents cannot afford the usual ornaments for the Christmas tree, buys pretty things for that purpose, paying for them with its own needles so that it becomes bare and ugly. The refrain is cumulative but always ends with the phrase, 'and the cookies bobbing about like little brown mice', which children love to join in with. There have been many beautiful poems about Christmas—look for them in such collections as James Reeves' *The Christmas Book*, an anthology of stories, poems and carols.

Finally, one international festival which should not be forgotten is Children's Book Day, inaugurated by the International Board on Books for Young People to commemorate Hans Andersen's birthday, 2nd April. This is obviously an occasion when children can hear some of Andersen's stories and something about his life which, in some aspects, is itself so like a fairy tale. It is an opportunity to remind children of 'The Ugly Duckling' (the real story—not the film version!), 'The Snow Queen' and 'The Emperor's New Clothes', stories no child should miss. Each year a different nation sponsors a poster by a national artist for the anniversary, and this is available in every country.

There are particular sections of the community which *need* stories, especially handicapped children in hospitals, children's homes and special schools. In hospitals long-term patients are often bored and lack mental stimulation, so that the arrival of a visitor from the outside world, particularly with a story, is always welcome. An appropriate time must be arranged with the hospital staff, of course, so that the storyteller does not interfere with hospital routine. The length and type of stories told will depend on the physical state of the patient. Visitors are often welcome in children's homes of various kinds by arrangement, to bring a new interest into the everyday routine, but the staff of these homes usually tell stories to their children as normal parents would.

Amongst the handicapped, I would make a special plea for storytelling to the blind, a group of which I have had some experience. These children are excitable, demonstrative and enjoy participation. Their reaction to a story is just as quick as that of a sighted child. There are difficulties, of course, for it has to be remembered that details of the story which one usually conveys by actions or facial expression must be translated into sound and words. I have found, however, that my greatest fear—that these children might not be able to form a mental picture of things they had never seen and which are taken for granted by sighted children—was unfounded. I do not know what they see when I speak of fields, flowers, the sky, for they rely so much on touch and sound, but undoubtedly it is something that satisfies them. As the story progresses, they clap their hands with excitement, jump up and ask, 'Did he get away? Is it going to be all right?' If I pause unduly, there will be anxious enquiries, 'Are you still there?' They need constant physical touch—I can still feel their fluttering fingers trace the outline of my face, and I will never forget one child's meditative comment as she did so—'I should think she's sixteen,' a supposition which, alas, was very far from the truth!

With physically handicapped children, you can tell stories as you would to any child. In my audience I have had spastics and children with muscular dystrophy so that half my listeners were in wheelchairs. Rather than selecting a 'special' story, I chose one about healthy children able to do adventurous things. A thalidomide child of three identified herself with the child I named after her in my story—for that brief space she *was* that other child with the use of all her limbs, and she beamed with delight.

Emotionally disturbed children are another matter. A story can be of help to a disturbed child, but there is always a danger that if the storyteller is ignorant of the particular problem, the story may upset the child. Storytelling for these children should only be undertaken with permission and expert advice. I have had such children in my audience sometimes (without my knowledge) and have been told that they listened with absorption, but it was simply my good fortune that the story I had chosen did not disturb them in any way.

Educationally subnormal children are another difficult audience, but here the 'reading age'—if there is one—is an indication of the type of story to tell, its level of difficulty and its length. Such children enjoy stories, but I have found it essential to tell them simply, not too quickly and with plenty of repetition. Pictures can be helpful, but too many may confuse the audience. In such cases, as with the others discussed in this chapter, the storyteller must be ready to adapt her stories to her audience. Extra care and thought in selecting and preparing the story is vital, but you can be assured that your efforts will be well rewarded.

IO

Storytelling—

Here and There

In the greater part of this book I have been discussing 'straight' storytelling, that is telling a story with no aid other than the voice and personality of the teller. Various aids can be used to supplement a story, but this is a different method of storytelling only to be used occasionally.

I have come across various ingenious schemes in schools aimed at introducing books and stories. In one, I saw teachers and children acting out fairy tales in the round, using narration, song and dance. The dialogue was largely impromptu, costume was only suggested, but the story grew before our eyes, a communal effort, gay and memorable. Another story, 'The Bear who wanted to be a Bird', had been set to music by a teacher to a guitar accompaniment. The children, the birds of the story, sang a mocking refrain. The project was an hilarious and exciting occasion for a large audience of children from schools in the neighbourhood. The stories had come to life in an unusual but traditional way.

Puppets—stringed, glove or finger—can be used effectively in presenting a story, especially to young children. The disadvantage of stringed puppets or marionettes is that they are complicated to make and require some skill to manipulate, besides needing a curtained off space behind which the operators can work, and a special kind of stage. However, produced as a co-operative effort between teachers or librarians, parents and children, these puppets can present stories in an entrancing and curiously lifelike way. I have found it easy to keep children absorbed for a programme of folk tales and interludes given by these puppets, but the equipment is cumbersome and the preparation and practice necessarily time consuming.

Glove puppets are familiar to all children and much simpler to make and use, with or without a portable stage and booth to hide the operator. They are a development of the ancient Punch and Judy shows, but any traditional story can be used according to the ingenuity of the puppeteers, often the children themselves. I often use a monkey puppet and I find that the fact that the audience *see* me put my hand inside the glove to animate him, does not detract from the illusion. Children will talk in whispers if I say he is tired, feed him with 'pretend' bananas (the real ones he finds indigestible) and after a story shake hands with him. As the children regard the puppet as a real person, I always tell a story in which he is the chief figure, a combination of my own imagination and some story about a monkey, for instance.

Finger puppets which fit individual fingers like a glove, can represent either people or animals. Finger puppets, one on each hand, can conduct a conversation, the three pigs can each have a finger on one hand, the wolf one on the other hand, for example. Simple nursery tales are suitable material. Because of the miniature size of such puppets, they can only be used with small groups.

Both these types of puppet involve children actively, either as operators or as a vociferous audience. A puppeteer usually invites children to warn him when the villain of the piece is approaching, a request which is always carried out with enthusiasm.

Television is regarded as a major source of stories for children and indeed both 'Jackanory' and 'Play School' have been the means of introducing many hundreds of books to children. I was one of the first storytellers on 'Play School' when it was started in 1964. In those days I was left free to tell a simple story in my own words without the aid of pictures. With the advent of colour television, it has become possible to present picture books in attractive and imaginative ways to young children, and today the story on 'Play School' usually comes from a picture book.

'Jackanory', in which I was also involved in its early days, used—and still does—a different method of telling stories from the one discussed in this book. When I gave a programme of Eleanor Farjeon's stories—and later *Mrs Pepperpot*—on 'Jackanory', I found I could not tell the stories as I would to children in the library, but had to read from a specially prepared script into which music and film had been interpolated. Today, more often than not, a whole book, rather than single stories, is read in parts by professional actors and actresses who are usually known to the public. Both these programmes suffer—from the point of view of the storyteller at least—from having to be presented not to children but to technicians and producers. It is claimed that this combination of vision and sound has brought back oral tradition, but the direct and *live* relationship between storyteller and child is still lacking and it is this which the kind of storytelling I have been advocating gives. I do not wish to decry an excellent programme, but this is not storytelling as I think of it.

Another way of telling a story is through film strips and cassettes on which voice, pictures and perhaps music are all a part of the story. The best selection is produced by Weston Woods Studios, who make cassettes and film strips of a variety of books, from the picture books of Charles Keeping and Brian Wildsmith to Beatrix Potter's 'Peter Rabbit' books, Gail E. Haley's *The Post Office Cat* and *The Five Chinese Brothers* by Claire Huchet Bishop. There are also films of Edward Ardizzone's *Little Tim and the Brave Sea Captain* and Isaac Bashevis Singer's 'Zlateh the Goat' among others. This type of storytelling is useful as a way of adding variety to a programme or when a live storyteller is not available. I have seen a group of young children watch Pat Hutchins' *Rosie's Walk* with its catchy tune three times over and still demand another showing.

Records or cassettes of stories *without* illustrations are of doubtful value for a group of children for there is no focal point to hold their attention. Uninterested children fidget and so distract those who do want to listen. The absence of a personal relationship is a drawback, for the faceless storyteller cannot, of course, adjust to this audience as a live storyteller would. However, an individual child can enjoy listening by himself, for this means that the story becomes a personal exchange between the unseen storyteller and the child. There is a wide range of stories available including *My Naughty Little Sister*, *Little Grey Rabbit*, some of Beatrix Potter's stories, *Winnie The Pooh*, a number of 'Jackanory' and 'Play School' stories and a variety of folk and fairy tales.

Films, cassettes, records, are all a somewhat artificial way of telling stories and can never be an adequate substitute for live storytelling. There is no limit to the ingenuity of imaginative *live* storytellers in the presentation of a story.

In Holland, a Dutch author, Margaret Bruijn, dressed as the traditional Mother Goose, talks about Perrault's fairy tales and tells stories herself, using the music of Ravel as a background. This fairy-tale programme has been enjoyed by hundreds of children in schools during the Dutch Annual Book Week and is both instructive and entertaining. In Canada I met a concert pianist who recited stories to music and two women who gave public recitals of African folk tales using drums as an accompaniment. In the United States two young women known as 'The Folktellers' tour the country as freelance storytellers. They tell stories, old and new, sometimes accompanied on the guitar, to children and adults at Folk Festivals and in libraries and schools; they also conduct workshops for teachers. These itinerant storytellers are reviving the old custom of taking stories to people everywhere.

Storytelling is still very much alive all over the world, particularly in the less sophisticated countries where people generally have more leisure time and fewer distractions than in the western world. Among the Eskimos, among the nomadic desert peoples, in the tropical islands of the South

Seas and on the shores of the Mediterranean, in the colourful markets of Africa and the bazaars of India, storytellers still pass on their national folk tales to the next generation. The Spider Man of the West Indian stories, the trolls and giants of Scandinavia, the Djins of Arabia, the fairy folk of Britain and the 'Baba Yagas' of Russia, are known to boys and girls of the twentieth century as they were to children centuries ago. In every country there are storytellers, unknown and unsung, who are keeping alive tradition by the age-old medium of storytelling. Parents, librarians, teachers and men and women from many walks of life who love stories, all play a part in the universal response to the children's demand 'Tell me a story!'

I believe that there are many members of the community who would be interested in telling stories to their own and other people's children (and to adults) given the encouragement, the opportunity and a little tuition. Fortunately there are many organisations and individuals all over the world who are doing much to promote interest in storytelling. In some parts of England, for example, librarians organise 'Family Reading Groups' in which parents are encouraged to read and tell stories and are advised on sources. One group of librarians recently organised a *ceilidh:* during the day there was storytelling for children and at night the adults enjoyed a 'Happy Evening' of stories, poems, music and songs such as is common in the West Indies and Haiti. This was an ideal way of sharing storytelling and singing; a community activity of this sort could give pleasure in other areas and do much to help keep alive oral tradition. When I was in Japan I was present at the regular monthly storytelling session for mothers run by the staff of the Tokyo Children's Library. I heard them tell 'Tom Tit Tot' (how did they translate the dialect?) and one of Eleanor Farjeon's stories. I know no Japanese, but the familiar stories were told so effectively that I could follow them easily. Storytelling was being fostered as a community activity enjoyed by adults and through them passed on to children.

The value of such occasions is largely due to the opportunities they offer for people to try storytelling themselves. They provide the vital stimulus which lectures in isolation can never give.

In Britain storytelling takes place in libraries, schools and the home and in many other, often unexpected, places through the enthusiasm of such organisations as the Federation of Books for Your Children Groups. Most libraries have regular story-sessions for pre-school children which are popular with both children and parents. Nowadays a number of libraries are taking books and stories outside the library walls.

In one London library, for instance, the staff and outside volunteers take books and stories to the places where children are likely to play during the summer holidays — parks, playgrounds, open spaces in an area of high-rise flats or housing estates where there is little feeling of community and children are often lonely. Such storytelling is very different from telling stories in a sheltered children's library. Often the environment is not conducive to listening and there are disruptive influences from uninterested older boys and girls. In many rural areas mobile libraries are parked on the village green at stated intervals during the school holidays and children gather there to borrow books and listen to stories.

Stories can be told anywhere if children want to listen. One year the Federation of Books for Your Children Groups chartered a train to carry hundreds of children from Birmingham to visit the London Book Fair. I was one of several authors who travelled with them — it was not an easy task to tell stories in a noisy train to a carriage full of excited children!

Adults, too, welcome an opportunity to hear stories. During the last decade it has become a tradition at the 'Loughborough' international course on children's literature to end the week with an evening of stories from the members' various cultures. Students at most conferences on children's literature find pleasure in informal storytelling as a natural accompaniment to their interest in children and books.

Story festivals can be exciting and inspiring occasions, especially when they involve representatives from all over the world. In 1956 such a festival was held as a part of the American Library Association Conference at Miami Beach. Storytellers from Japan, Germany, the West Indies, Ireland, the southern states of America and Britain (myself) gave a programme to a large audience of professional librarians and *one* child (who had been smuggled in by her mother). The stories were told against an exotic background of hibiscus, oleanders, sea-grapes and magnolia. No one could doubt the enjoyment of the adults listening to stories usually reserved for children. Another notable story festival is the one held occasionally at Boys' and Girls' House, Toronto, a library where there has always been storytelling since Lillian Smith, the eminent children's librarian, introduced the tradition in the first half of this century. These festivals were founded in 1961 at the request of John Masefield and I was his representative during a whole week of storytelling for young and old. At a recent festival in Toronto, the programme included the three ways of telling stories, in speech, song and dance. Indian children in tribal dress told a traditional story in dance and mime, accompanied on drums; a folk-singer sang sea-shanties which embodied a tale; expert storytellers told folk tales from different cultures.

In schools there are many opportunities for telling stories. Naturally, storytelling is used most in the infant school, although again it is a fallacy to think that only the youngest children enjoy listening to a well-told story. Sadly, even in the infants' department many teachers read stories rather than tell them. I believe that every teacher should receive some tuition and encouragement in telling stories during their training, but this is not always the case.

I was a lecturer on one 'refresher' course for teachers which was specifically planned to encourage the telling of stories in schools. Several teachers told stories most effectively, and the inspector in charge entranced the group with an hilarious story of his own invention. It was obvious that, given encouragement, most people can tell stories.

Children, too, can become excellent storytellers, but because of their lack of experience in expressing themselves in this way before their peers, they can become confused and incoherent. This is tedious for the audience who want to know what happens next. It is advisable, therefore, to run through the chosen story with the child beforehand so that he has more confidence in his ability to tell it when he faces other children. Some children have a flair for telling stories and feel no diffidence about it. I remember one girl of ten who told an episode from *Charlotte's Web* with an astonishing wealth of detail and considerable dramatic effect. Why not encourage children to become the storytellers of the future? I participated in one imaginative project involving one hundred and twenty children in storytelling, poetry and art. The children were inspired to write stories themselves and to illustrate those they had heard. Later they were to retell the stories they liked to their schoolmates. It was a happy and stimulating experience for everyone concerned.

I cannot do better than conclude with a poet and storyteller's vision of what storytelling might be. John Masefield was himself a wonderful storyteller and at one time he told a 'set' of stories to hundreds of audiences in this country and others. It convinced him that men and women enjoy stories and can be deeply moved by them. He made many attempts to introduce storytelling to the public, enlisting the help of schools of drama only to find they turned stories into plays. He planned to form a Guild of Storytellers who would bring stories to people everywhere, but this never materialised.

What was it he longed to see as part of his lifetime search for beauty? He visualised groups of musicians, singers, dancers and practised storytellers, wearing costumes of 'strangeness and beauty'. The storytellers would tell the story in turn and there would be interludes of music and dance to add splendour and excitement. So in a tale of three tasks to be done by the hero, the magic of the doing could be suggested in dance and mime, the triumphant completion announced by a Messenger as in Greek drama. The storytelling would be presented 'in the round' on a low platform so that the audience became part of the story.

Alas! Such storytelling as this has never been achieved. Nevertheless, there have always been storytellers and always will be in every generation, to delight children by passing on the old, old stories 'told newly, told memorably, told again'.

Book List

The following list of books is merely intended to indicate the source of the stories mentioned in the text. It is in no sense a comprehensive list of recommended books.

PICTURE STORY BOOKS

The 'Babar' books Jean de Brunhoff (Methuen)

Charley, Charlotte and the Golden Canary Charles Keeping (Oxford University Press)

The Elephant and the Bad Baby Elfrida Vipont (Hamish Hamilton/Puffin paperback)

The Five Chinese Brothers Claire Huchet Bishop (Bodley Head)

Gone is Gone Wanda Gag (Faber/Puffin paperback)

The Good Little Christmas Tree Ursula Moray Williams (Hamish Hamilton)

The 'Gumdrop' books Val Biro (Hodder & Stoughton/Piccolo paperback)

Harry the Dirty Dog Margaret Bloy Graham (Bodley Head/Puffin paperback)

Millions of Cats Wanda Gag (Faber/Puffin paperback)

'Mr Gumpy' books John Burningham (Cape/Puffin paperback)

The Post Office Cat Gail E. Haley (Bodley Head/Methuen paperback)

Rosie's Walk Pat Hutchins (Bodley Head/Puffin paperback)

The Story of the Little Red Engine Diana Ross (Faber)

The Three Robbers Tomi Ungerer (Methuen)

The Tiger who came to tea Judith Kerr (Collins/Lion paperback)

The 'Tim' books   Edward Ardizzone   (Oxford University Press)

NURSERY RHYMES, BALLADS AND POEMS
A Bundle of Ballads   Ruth Manning-Sanders   (Oxford University Press)
Cautionary Tales   Hilaire Belloc   (Duckworth)
A Child's Garden of Verses   Robert Louis Stevenson   (many editions)
'Did you Feed my Cow?' in *A Second Storyteller's Choice*   Eileen Colwell   (Bodley Head)
Figgie Hobbin   Charles Causley   (Macmillan/Puffin paperback)
Four Feet and Two   Leila Berg   (Puffin paperback)
'I went to the Animal Fair' in *The Magic Umbrella and Other Stories for Telling*   Eileen Colwell   (Bodley Head)
'hist whist' e. e. cummings   in *Humblepuppy and Other Stories for Telling*   Eileen Colwell   (Bodley Head)
Nicola Bayley's Book of Nursery Rhymes   (Cape)
The Puffin Book of Nursery Rhymes   Iona and Peter Opie   (Puffin paperback)
Rhyme Time   Barbara Ireson   (Hamlyn/Beaver paperback)
Shadows and Spells   Barbara Ireson   (Faber)
Silly Verse for Kids   Spike Milligan   (Dobson/Puffin paperback)
This Little Pig Went to Market   Norah Montgomerie   (Bodley Head)
This Little Puffin   Elizabeth Matterson   (Puffin paperback)
'What did you put in your Pocket?'   Beatrice Schenk de Regniers   in *Humblepuppy*   Eileen Colwell   (Bodley Head)

STORIES TO BE FOUND IN SHORT-STORY COLLECTIONS
The Adventures of Tim Rabbit   Alison Uttley   (Faber/Puffin paperback)

78

'Bertha Goldfoot' in *The Old Nurse's Stocking-Basket*
Eleanor Farjeon (Oxford University Press)
A Book of Ghosts and Goblins Ruth Manning-Sanders
(Methuen/Piccolo paperback)
The Christmas Book James Reeves (Heinemann)
'The Dog that Had No Name' in *Lollipops* Leila
Berg (Hodder & Stoughton)
'The Elephant's Picnic' in *Don't Blame Me* Richard
Hughes (Chatto & Windus)
'Elsie Piddock Skips in her Sleep' in *Martin Pippin in the
Daisy Field* Eleanor Farjeon (Oxford University
Press)
The Goalkeeper's Revenge Bill Naughton (Heinemann
Educ.)
A Hallowe'en Acorn Eileen Colwell (Bodley Head)
'Humblepuppy' in *A Harp of Fishbones* Joan Aiken
(Cape)
Just So Stories Rudyard Kipling (Macmillan/Piccolo
paperback)
'A Meal with a Magician' in *My Friend Mr Leakey*
J. B. S. Haldane (Puffin paperback)
'Milly-Molly-Mandy' stories Joyce Brisley
(Harrap/Puffin paperback)
'Mrs Pepperpot' books Alf Proysen (Hutchinson/Puffin
paperback)
'My Naughty Little Sister' books Dorothy Edwards
(Methuen/Puffin paperback)
'Ponder and William' stories Barbara Softly (Puffin
paperback)
'The Quacking Pillarbox' in *Some Time Stories* Donald
Bisset (Methuen)
The Sam Pig Storybook Alison Uttley (Faber)
'Schnitzle, Schnotzle, and Schnootzle' in *The Long
Christmas* Ruth Sawyer (Bodley Head)
The Shadow-Cage and Other Tales of the Supernatural
Philippa Pearce (Kestrel/Puffin paperback)

Tales of Arabel's Raven   Joan Aiken   (Jackanory Story Books, B.B.C./Cape)

Tom Tit Tot and Other Stories   (Jackanory Story Books, B.B.C.)

'Zlateh the Goat'   in *Zlateh the Goat and Other Stories*   Isaac Bashevis Singer   (Kestrel)

FOLK TALES, FAIRY TALES AND LEGENDS

Abbey Lubbers, Banshees and Boggarts: A Who's Who of Fairies   Katharine Briggs   (Kestrel)

'Aesop' fables   (many editions)

Animal Folk Tales Around the World   Kathleen Arnott   (Blackie)

'Baba Yaga'   in *Old Peter's Russian Tales*   Arthur Ransome   (Puffin paperback)

Baron Munchausen and Other Comic Tales from Germany   R. E. Raspe   (Dent)

Beowulf: Dragon Slayer   Rosemary Sutcliff   (Bodley Head/Puffin paperback)

Beowulf the Warrior   Ian Serraillier   (Oxford University Press)

'The Birth of Oisin'   in *The High Deeds of Finn Mac Cool*   Rosemary Sutcliff   (Bodley Head/Puffin paperback)

A Book of Sorcerers and Spells   *A Book of Witches*   both by Ruth Manning-Sanders   (Methuen/Piccolo paperback)

Brer Rabbit Stories   (Jackanory Story Books, B.B.C.)

'Brother Johannick and his Silver Bell'   in *Tales of Jack and Jane*   Elizabeth Clark   (U.L.P.)

The Burning of Njal   Henry Treece   (Bodley Head)

Celtic Fairy Tales   Joseph Jacobs   (Bodley Head)

The Chronicles of Robin Hood   Rosemary Sutcliff   (Oxford University Press)

The Faber Book of North American Legends   Virginia Haviland   (Faber)

The Faber Book of Northern Legends   K. Crossley-Holland   (Faber)

80

Fairy Tales Hans Andersen (many editions)
'Fierce Feathers' L. V. Hodgkin in *The Magic Umbrella*
  Eileen Colwell (Bodley Head)
'The Gorgon's Head' in *The Heroes* Charles
  Kingsley (Dent)
Grettir the Strong Allen French (Bodley Head)
The High Deeds of Finn Mac Cool Rosemary
  Sutcliff (Bodley Head/Puffin paperback)
'The Hobyahs' in *English Fairy Tales* Joseph
  Jacobs (Bodley Head)
The Hound of Ulster Rosemary Sutcliff (Bodley Head)
'The Jolly Tailor who Became King' L. M. Borski in
  A Storyteller's Choice Eileen Colwell (Bodley Head)
King Arthur and His Knights of the Round Table Roger
  Lancelyn Green (Puffin paperback)
The Light Beyond the Forest Rosemary Sutcliff (Bodley
  Head/Knight paperback)
'The Magic Kettle' in *Stories from Everywhere* Rhoda
  Power (Dobson)
'Molly Whuppie' in *English Fairy Tales* Joseph
  Jacobs (Bodley Head)
'Mr Fox' in *English Fairy Tales*
Myths of the Norsemen Roger L. Green (Puffin paperback)
'Nix Nought Nothing' in *English Fairy Tales* (Bodley
  Head)
'The Selfish Giant' in *Fairy Tales* Oscar
  Wilde (Bodley Head)
'The Sleeping Beauty' in *Fairy Book* Arthur
  Rackham (Harrap)
Tales of Magic and Enchantment Alison Uttley, ed.
  Kathleen Lines (Faber)
'The Three Sillies' in *English Fairy Tales* (Bodley
  Head)
'To Your Good Health' in *Favourite Fairy Tales Told In
  Russia* Virginia Haviland (Bodley Head)
'The Turnip' in *Stories to Tell* Elizabeth
  Clark (Hodder & Stoughton/Piccolo paperback)

'Two of Everything' in *The Treasure of Li-Po* Alice
Ritchie (Hogarth Press)
'Volkh's Journey to the East' E. M. Almedingen in
The Knights of the Golden Table and in *A Second Storyteller's
Choice* (Bodley Head)
'Where Arthur Sleeps' in *Welsh Legends and
Folk-Tales* Gwyn Jones (Oxford University Press)
'The Witch and the Swan Maiden' in *The Glass Man and
the Golden Bird* Ruth Manning-Sanders (Oxford
University Press)

STORIES TO BE FOUND IN STORYTELLING
COLLECTIONS

'The Bear who wanted to be a Bird' A. & C. De
Leeuw in *Tell Me Another Story* Eileen
Colwell (Puffin paperback)
'A Chinese Fairy Tale' Laurence Housman in *A
Storyteller's Choice* Eileen Colwell (Bodley Head)
'The Golden Phoenix' Marius Barbeau in *A Second
Storyteller's Choice* Eileen Colwell (Bodley Head)
'Lazy Tok' Mervyn Skipper in *A Storyteller's
Choice* Eileen Colwell (Bodley Head)
'The Little Pagan Faun' Patrick Chalmers in *A
Storyteller's Choice* Eileen Colwell (Bodley Head)
'The Magic Umbrella' Rose Fyleman in *The Magic
Umbrella and Other Stories for Telling* Eileen
Colwell (Bodley Head)
Playtime Stories Joyce Donoghue (Puffin paperback)
A Second Storyteller's Choice Eileen Colwell (Bodley
Head)
'The Signalman' Charles Dickens in *The Magic
Umbrella and Other Stories for Telling* Eileen
Colwell (Bodley Head)
Tales Told Again Walter de la Mare (Faber)
'The Three Sleeping Boys of Warwickshire' Walter de
la Mare in *Collected Stories for Children* (Faber)
The Youngest Storybook Eileen Colwell (Bodley Head)

OTHER BOOKS FROM WHICH STORIES CAN BE TOLD

The Adventures of Sajo and Her Beaver People 'Grey
  Owl' (Heinemann Educ.)
The Boy Who Was Afraid Armstrong Sperry (Bodley
  Head)
The Bullerby Children Astrid Lindgren (Methuen)
Charlotte's Web E. B. White (Hamish Hamilton/Puffin
  paperback)
Emil and the Detectives Erich Kästner (Cape/Puffin
  paperback)
The Family from One End Street Eve Garnett
  (Heinemann/Puffin paperback)
The Ivory Horn Ian Serraillier (Oxford University
  Press)
Jim Davis John Masefield (Puffin paperback)
The King of the Copper Mountains Paul Biegel (Dent)
The Mousewife Rumer Godden (Macmillan)
Nurse Matilda Christianna Brand (Hodder & Stoughton)
The Phoenix and the Carpet E. Nesbit (Benn/Puffin
  paperback)
The Water Babies Charles Kingsley (Dent)
Winnie the Pooh A. A. Milne (Methuen)

ABOUT STORYTELLING
The Art of the Storyteller Marie Shedlock (Dover
  Publications)
Children and Stories Antony Jones and June
  Buttrey (Blackwell)
An Old Woman's Reflections Peig Sayers (Oxford
  University Press)
The Ordinary and the Fabulous Elizabeth Cook
  (Cambridge University Press)
The Way of the Storyteller Ruth Sawyer (Bodley Head)